Empire
and
Interest

*The American Colonies and the
Politics of Mercantilism*

PILOTBOOKS

DEALING WITH SIGNIFICANT QUESTIONS
FROM THE AMERICAN PAST

Under the Editorship of

Lawrence H. Leder, Lehigh University
Norman K. Risjord, University of Wisconsin
Walter T. K. Nugent, Indiana University

Published in

THE LIPPINCOTT HISTORY SERIES

Under the Editorship of

Robert F. Byrnes, Indiana University
Robert D. Cross, Swarthmore College

Empire
and
Interest

*The American Colonies
and the Politics of Mercantilism*

by MICHAEL KAMMEN
CORNELL UNIVERSITY

J. B. LIPPINCOTT COMPANY

*Philadelphia
New York
Toronto*

Preface

The work of Sir Lewis Namier (1888-1960) has had a profound impact upon historical scholarship in Britain and America. His more than thirty years of remarkable research and writing substantially altered our understanding of politics and society in Georgian England and stimulated many contributions by avowed and unavowed "Namierites" (as well as "anti-Namierites"). Whatever they are called, and broadly considered, they are not a school, their collective output has been a barrage of books and essays on eighteenth-century Britain and the First Empire. American scholars, particularly colonial historians and those interested in the Age of the American Revolution, have noted Namier's and his successors' contributions and have incorporated them into their interpretations.

Nonetheless it is remarkable that a new approach—more than a synthesis—has not emerged: one that would relate the contributions of Namier and the *epigoni*, not only to American colonial history, but to the early history of the industrial revolution in Britain, to the incredible flood of writings in the later eighteenth century on political economy, and to the dynamics (as opposed to Namier's essentially static picture) of English society, public life, and the Empire in these years. I have attempted to suggest such an approach in the extended essay which follows. In doing so I am heartened by Dr. J. H. Plumb's recent observation that "a new analytic materialism is putting down strong roots, and we can expect the sort of renaissance that France has enjoyed since Marc Bloch."

With Bloch, and the poet Valéry, I realize that "the great day of definitions, of distinct and special terms, to replace those of confused . . . origin, has not yet arrived for history." I have tried, nevertheless, to make clear from the outset what mercantilism meant to contemporaries, what "interest" and "interests" meant to the eighteenth-century mind, and what "interest group" means to the modern political scientist. A discussion of those concepts in historical context occupies much of Chapter 1, along with a formulation of my major theme, particularly with reference to the years before 1660. Chapters 2 and 3 treat what I have loosely called "Interests in Equilibrium (1660-1696)" and "The Age of Walpole (1696-1748)," during which the nature of mercantilism, the British economy, and the role of interests in imperial affairs gradually underwent significant alterations. Chapter 4 analyzes fifteen years of stunningly rapid transformation (1748-1762), and suggests that circumstances of peace after 1748, as much as conditions of war after 1756, helped precipitate the revolutionary crisis. The following two chapters deal with the period 1763-1783. Chapter 5 examines those two decades as "An Age of Interests," discussing British and imperial politics in terms of the dominant role played by some fifty to sixty interest groups in public affairs. Chapter 6 analyzes the same era from the particular perspective of the American colonies and the great imperial crisis. The Epilogue looks briefly at the changing nature and role of interest groups in British and American politics after 1783.

Readers will note that my essay is both selective and interpretative. Well-known aspects in the narrative of Anglo-American history are treated lightly, almost taken for granted. Readers seeking greater detail about a particular episode or trend in imperial history will wish to consult some of the titles suggested in the Bibliographical Essay.

My objective throughout has been to explore and explain the political economy of an empire in terms of its complex and diverse social groups. In pursuing that goal I have become persuaded that "interests," as both eighteenth- and twentieth-century observers understand that term, were vitally important (and subsequently much neglected) units of activity and influence. Yet to index and measure the power and inter-action of groups is not easy where one confronts diverse com-mercial, religious, social, local, and bureaucratic interests, as well as such latent political forces as labor. The success of any given interest depended upon its organization, influence, and finances; upon the government's needs and weaknesses at the moment; and upon which other groups were then active and aggressive. Moreover, the personal attributes of lobbyists were more important in the eighteenth century than today, because the interests they represented were less firmly institutionalized, and because personal relationships in Georgian England were at the very heart of politics.

Those interests which produced formal associations often achieved a special stability, simply because organization con-tributes to continuity. I have paid extra attention to this matter in Chapter 3. Interest groups commonly seek to develop and improve their access to power. In doing so they may try to exclude competitive groups from equivalent access to pres-sure points important in the decision-making process. This problem and its particular impact upon the American colonies forms a special concern of Chapter 5. Finally, an interest's strategic position among other groups, the character of its overlapping attachments, and the skills and social standing of its spokesmen largely determine that group's cohesion and abil-ity to succeed. The deference paid to a respected group facili-tates acceptance of its arguments and eases its approach to government. These last concerns are central to my discussion of the North American interest in Chapter 6.

For most of our lengthy period we shall be examining an empire that was closely knit in economic conception but loosely administered in reality. What relationship, we must ask, was there between that anomaly and the pervasive activity of inter-est groups in domestic and imperial politics? Finally, what does the changing relationship between these elements tell us about the origins of the American Revolution? An answer was sug-gested by John Brown, an English pamphleteer, when he wrote in 1757 that "a *Chain* of *Self-Interest* is indeed no better than a *Rope of Sand:* There is no *Cement* nor *Cohesion* between the Parts: There is rather a mutual *Antipathy* and *Repulsion.*"

Once again my wife has helped with the research, combed and brushed several versions of the manuscript. Bernard Bailyn, F. J. Levy, and Richard B. Morris read an earlier and much briefer rendition, improving it by their criticisms. Thomas C. Barrow, Hugh F. Bell, Robert F. Byrnes, Clive Holmes, Jack P. Greene, Lawrence H. Leder, and Joel H. Silbey scrutinized the final copy; I am deeply grateful for their thoughtfulness and insights. Felix Reichmann, "Grand Acquisitor" of the Cornell University Library, has helped in many ways, as have Mary T. Menke, Steven T. Cresap, and Robert Ritchie, editor extraordinary at J. B. Lippincott.

M. K.

Ithaca, New York
July 4, 1969

Contents

Louis XIV. By Christmas of 1688, James had thrown the Great Seal into the Thames and fled to France. William had entered London. Again a Convention Parliament met and eventually offered the crown to William and Mary jointly. In the subsequent year, a series of parliamentary enactments made the first constitutional adjustments necessitated by the Glorious Revolution. The last decade of the seventeenth century brought further changes, culminating in 1701 in the Act of Settlement.

As a result of that Act, the crown would eventually shift from the last Stuarts (William died in 1702; and Anne, second daughter of James II, reigned until her death in August, 1714) to the German House of Hanover, linked to the Stuarts by marriage through a granddaughter of James I. On September 18, 1714, George I landed in England and formed a new government. A year later a Jacobite uprising in Scotland failed. James III, Stuart pretender to the throne, fled and thereby assured the Hanoverian succession. Forty years of comparatively stable government followed—stability that perhaps owed more to Sir Robert Walpole's administrative control, 1721-1742, than to the royal courts of George I (1714-1727) and his son George II (1727-1760). Walpole prided himself upon his success in keeping Britain detached from continental intrigues and wars. England had fought with Holland in 1664-1667 and again in 1672-1674. From 1689 until 1697, and again from 1702 until 1713, England actively engaged in European military alliances against Louis XIV of France. For twenty-six years thereafter, however, peace endured, ended in 1739 by the memorable War of Jenkins' Ear which lingered on until 1748.

The British Empire, meanwhile, had expanded in extraordinary ways. In 1660 two Chesapeake colonies, twice as many New England colonies, and some tiny Caribbean dependencies were desperately seeking economic viability and political stability. They were threatened on the south and west by the Spanish, on the north and west by French and Indians. A century later, in 1763, Britain's grasp embraced North America from Rupert's Land to Florida, and the eastern hemisphere from Gibraltar to Bengal. The number, size, and strength of its imperial dependencies had grown immeasurably, and its international prestige had increased accordingly. During the reign of Charles II, both Carolinas, East and West Jersey, Pennsylvania, and New Hampshire all came into being; New Netherland became New York by conquest, and the Caribbean colonies grew in number and value. Strategic and philanthropic impulses converged in 1730 to give birth to Georgia. And British military successes in 1758-1759 tolled the death knell for New France. Canada formally became a British possession in 1763. A vast empire had come to be.

It brought with it serious problems, problems of territorial and financial administration at a time when Britain was in fiscal difficulty. The factionalism and instability characteristic of British politics in the 1760's made it even more difficult to establish and enforce a workable policy for the American colonies. Consequently, misunderstanding on both sides, British tactical blunders, and America's compulsive concern with liberty and conspiracy helped produce a series of crises. They culminated finally in the Boston Tea Party late in 1773. Then came independence in 1776, the military struggle, and peacemaking in 1782-1783. Thereafter England underwent a brief era of administrative reform before plunging into a quarter-century of war with France. In 1801 the legislative union of Great Britain and Ireland completed a process begun in 1707 with Scotland. The new United Kingdom presented the world with a consolidated unity at home to replace the thirteen missing members across the sea. An empire had been altered. So had the imperial attitudes of many of its dominant politicians, who had known only the maddeningly long reign of George III (1760-1820).

Yet the formal history of Britain and its Empire after 1660 merely suggests reigns of monarchs, violent wars, and external changes in constitutional arrangements. There were also formal and informal patterns of thought shaping the course of Empire, as well as formally and informally organized social groups, economic associations, and political organizations. Many of them, for example, were responsible for England's century-long commercial war with France. It began with an act of Parliament in 1678, placing an embargo on all French wine, vinegar, brandy, linen, cloth, silk, salt, paper and any manufactures containing thread, wool, hair, gold, silver, or leather. It did not end until the Treaty of Eden in 1786.

THE NATURE OF ENGLISH MERCANTILISM

Mercantilism as a concept or system was a will-o'-the-wisp. It meant different things at different times and in different places. English mercantile thought in 1620 was unlike both French mercantile thought in 1620 and English thought in 1720. Even so, we should at least attempt to establish a meaningful cluster of associations with the term "mercantilism," for like humanism, equally elusive, it was nevertheless an important consideration in the minds of men.

It has since become a vague term, suggesting perhaps the opposite of laissez-faire, as well as many more misleading ideas. Surprisingly the word was unknown in the seventeenth century and for most of the eighteenth. The phrase "mercantile system" only became commonplace in the writings of Adam Smith. Thereafter it acquired popular usage and was much discussed among nineteenth-century intellectuals and politicians. They well remembered Smith's strong opposition to "the mercantile system." In his view, it was a commercial minority's scheme to gain a monopoly of the home market for manufacturers by regulating trade, and, ostensibly, to secure a favorable balance in the national interest.

Perhaps the most distinguished student of mercantilism since Adam Smith is Professor Eli Heckscher whose great work, *Mercantilism*, appeared in Sweden in 1931 and three years later in an English translation.[1] Heckscher's profound and influential study followed many nineteenth-century economic theorists in emphasizing power as a primary element in mercantilism, but unlike his predecessors Heckscher condemned rather than

---

[1] Eli F. Heckscher, *Mercantilism* (London, 1935), 2 vols.

praised that emphasis. Heckscher saw a reasonably uniform system of economic thought and practice in early modern Europe, a system characterized by a certain conception of society, a desire for national unification, for economic protection, for the accumulation of treasure, and—above all—for the pursuit of power. His views have been controversial, but they remain the last full-scale exploration and analysis of the problem. What, we must now ask, did mercantilism, or its component ideas, mean in Tudor and Stuart England?

Mercantilism had much to do with men's conception of the balance of trade. From the mid-sixteenth century until the mid-eighteenth—the so-called Age of Mercantilism—men were not allowed to export materials needed by clothiers and other manufacturers, the export of coin and bullion was forbidden, and many legislative acts encouraged English shipping.[2] "A growing consciousness of the corporate character of the nation-state," Professor Charles Wilson has written, "combined perhaps with contemporary scientific notions of equilibrium," turned the balance of trade into a popular gauge of economic welfare. As one Elizabethan put it: "If we send out more comodities in valeu than we bring home . . . the overpluis must nedes be paid for in moneye, and this is the measure of increasinge or diminishinge the Coyne, except of that little which is found within the realme." A favorable balance meant the acquisition of treasure: easy to carry in relation to value, imperishable, acceptable everywhere, and readily divisible.[3]

Two generations later these notions would be reiterated in Thomas Mun's *Englands Treasure by Fforraign Trade*, a work which quickly became established orthodoxy for later mercantilists. A favorable balance and acquisition of bullion involved the salient risks, understood by economic theorists, of inflation and hampered competition in export markets. Even

---

[2] B. Suviranta, *The Theory of the Balance of Trade in England: A Study in Mercantilism* (Helsingfors, 1923).

[3] Charles Wilson, *Mercantilism* (London, 1958), pp. 10-11.

so, an unfavorable balance posed a still graver threat to the national welfare.[4]

Mercantilist writers were not simply ivory-tower philosophers speculating on the abstract functioning of an unreal system. Gradually their conception of the balance of trade was absorbed into seventeenth-century legislation. By the 1620's—a decade of depression—economic thought and governmental policy had become intertwined. Thomas Mun and his colleagues set forth in six major principles what became the essence of mercantilist policy for a century.

1. English raw materials should be reserved to the cloth industry by prohibiting the export of wool, fuller's earth, pipe clay, and other necessities, especially to Holland.

2. English ships and merchants should not be allowed to supply Dutch competitors with Spanish or Turkish wool.

3. The need for imports and loss of bullion should be reduced by developing manufactures; producing linen, hemp, and flax at home would make England independent of the Baltic.

4. The Dutch should be ousted from the fisheries and supplanted by the English.

5. Foreign merchants and shipmasters who earned money in England as importers should be required to spend their earnings on English manufactures.

6. Goods imported from abroad should come either in English ships or those of the country producing the goods.

Taken together these desiderata constituted an attack on the lucrative role of the Dutch in Europe's economy. The attack was rationalized by economic nationalism; its goal was a favorable balance of trade.

---

[4] R. W. K. Hinton, "The Mercantile System in the Time of Thomas Mun," *Economic History Review*, 2nd ser., VII (1955), 277-90.

Beyond that sanctified concept lay another which seems naïve today, but not to seventeenth-century minds. They cherished the acquisition of precious metals which they believed necessary to maintain a sound and adequate currency. Whenever economic crises threatened, men feared that "a scarcity of coin" would slow the volume of trade and cause a depression. Undeniably, some branches of foreign trade required sizeable supplies of precious metal. This was true in the purchasing of Baltic corn during the first half of the seventeenth century and of timber and naval stores for shipbuilding in the second half. The East India Company exported large quantities of silver in order to purchase spices from the East. Perhaps the mercantilists' preoccupation with "treasure" was fairly grounded in the economic circumstances of seventeenth-century Europe.

In summary, despite differences and considerable vagueness of detail among writers of Stuart England, a body of opinion, both official and informal, held that England's national power and wealth depended upon its development as a strong maritime and commercial nation, constantly seeking to enlarge its foreign trade in the hope of achieving a favorable balance. These were not new ideas. English merchants, often with governmental approval, had long envisaged national wealth in terms of trade. Under the Stuarts, however, and especially after 1660, there was greater overall planning, a stronger emphasis upon industrial output, along with an increased consciousness of international rivalries and the strategic maneuvering they required. Essentially, the English envied the Dutch, feared the French, and were eager to seduce the Spanish and Portuguese.[5]

The mercantile system, as Professor Wilson has written,

---

[5] Mildred Campbell, " 'Of People Either Too Few or Too Many.' The Conflict of Opinion on Population and Its Relation to Emigration," in William A. Aiken and Basil D. Henning, eds., *Conflict in Stuart England: Essays in Honour of Wallace Notestein* (New York, 1960), pp. 187-88.

"was composed of all the devices, legislative, administrative and regulatory, by which societies still predominantly agrarian sought to transform themselves into trading and industrial societies, to equip themselves not only to be rich but to be strong, and to remain so."[6] The great age of English mercantilism, from late Elizabethan times until early Georgian, was one of remarkably rapid economic expansion, especially by comparison with what had gone before. The mercantilists may have been shortsighted in some respects. Their motives, logic, morals, methods, and behavior may have often been reprehensible. But, above all, their purposes were immediate and far from theoretical in any detached and academic sense. They viewed economic processes and institutions in their political context; so now must we.

The Nature and Role of Interests

When examining the operations of the Hudson's Bay Company in the later seventeenth century or the South Sea Company in the early eighteenth, it is often difficult to separate organizational aspirations from governmental policies. Both companies, for example, participated directly in their government's diplomatic negotiations concerning areas of America in which they were interested. Essentially, it was the private economic groups' seeking to determine state and imperial policies that shaped mercantilism.

Interest groups have led rather shadowy lives in histories of seventeenth- and eighteenth-century British and imperial politics. Much is known about particular interests, and many groups, as well as the term "interest"—used in various ways—repeatedly appear in the literature. Nonetheless, their cumulative significance in public affairs, their collective role in the "System of politicks," and their relationship to major events—such as the American Revolution—remain unclear and undeter-

---

6 Wilson, *Mercantilism*, pp. 26-27.

mined. In short, we need a comprehensive analysis of the role played by interest groups in the Anglo-American world.[7]

Sir Lewis Namier's emphasis upon family connections and parliamentary interests, as he called them, only perplexes in this context because Namier's recognition of "the absence of organized parties" in Georgian England led him to a fragmented view of the essential units competing for favor and power. In reacting to traditional interpretations of eighteenth-century politics, he perhaps went too far, reducing the dynamic elements in public life to individuals, families, and "circles which are primarily concerned with the nation's political business and form therefore the political nation."[8] In his own work and in that of scholars closely associated with him, these circles are referred to as interests.[9] While such terminol-

---

[7] At best we have a textbook by Professor Dorothy Marshall in which interests provide a recurrent though haphazard theme, a brilliant general essay by Samuel H. Beer on "The Representation of Interests in British Government," and several new books sensitive to the primary importance of interests as determinants of public policy. See Dorothy Marshall, *Eighteenth Century England* (London, 1962); and Beer in *American Political Science Review*, LI (1957), 613-50, reprinted as chap. 1 in *British Politics in the Collectivist Age* (New York, 1965). Two astute historians drop casual references to the significant role played by interest groups in the eighteenth century. See Perry Miller, *The New England Mind From Colony to Province* (Cambridge, Mass., 1953), p. ix; Harold Nicolson, *The Age of Reason (1700-1789)* (London, 1960), p. 175.

[8] *The Structure of Politics at the Accession of George III* (2d ed.; London, 1960), pp. 133-34; *Personalities and Powers* (London, 1955), p. 43; [with John Brooke]: *The History of Parliament: The House of Commons, 1754-1790* (London, 1964), I, 109; Robert Walcott, " 'Sir Lewis Namier Considered' Considered," *Journal of British Studies*, III (1964), 99. I do not mean to suggest that Namier was insensitive to the role of interest groups. He devoted considerable attention to the West Indian interest and to a number of lesser ones. But they were not of primary importance to him, and he never developed a comprehensive explanation of their place in eighteenth-century politics.

[9] Namier and Brooke, *The History of Parliament. The House of Commons, 1754-1790*, I, 46 ff.; Robert Walcott, *English Politics in the Early Eighteenth Century* (Oxford, 1956), pp. 110-11, 125; Archibald S. Foord, *His Majesty's Opposition, 1714-1830* (Oxford, 1964), pp. 21-22, 45, 49-50, 60, 69, 89-90, 118, 134, 136, 141, 164, 177, 276, 281, 307-8. A notable exception occurs on pp. 194-95, where Foord refers to the configuration of economic interest groups during the ministry of Sir Robert Walpole.

ogy (and there are also numerous references to "the government interest" in this context) is unexceptionable, it has created a false similarity because these family-oriented electoral and parliamentary interests correspond neither with our own understanding of interest groups nor with the considerable numbers of such groups that were active in eighteenth-century politics.[10]

Local electoral interests may have been important in early modern England. But to attain a balanced view we must also give proper attention to factions and factionalism—that pejoratively regarded condition that exists when the party system breaks down. Between 1675 and 1775 there were parties during certain periods and factions during others (and in the past forty years, especially, historians have charted their checkered history in staggering detail). But interest groups *constantly* existed: some manifest and some latent, some articulate and some inarticulate, some formally organized and some merely "a condition of like-mindedness and informal communication about issues."[11] As the political scientist Gabriel Almond has pointed out, the kinds of interest groups which are present in a society, the specificity or diffuseness of their demands, their conceptions of the political arena and of the "rules of the game," the ethos which they bring with them into the political process—these are the "raw materials" of politics—the unaggregated demands which some set of mechanisms must transform into public policy.

Robert MacIver, another political scientist, has provided a useful and general definition of interests: "When a number of men unite for the defense, maintenance or enhancement of any

[10] *Cf.* Lewis M. Wiggin, *The Faction of Cousins: A Political Account of the Grenvilles, 1733-1763* (New Haven, 1958). S. E. Finer is one of the very few political scientists or historians to recognize that eighteenth-century Englishmen had a special and rather modern conception of interests. See "Interest Groups and the Political Process in Great Britain," in Henry W. Ehrmann, ed., *Interest Groups on Four Continents* (Pittsburgh, 1958), p. 117.

[11] See the superb theoretical analysis of Gabriel A. Almond, "A Comparative Study of Interest Groups and the Political Process," *American Political Science Review*, LII (1958), 270-82.

more or less enduring position or advantage which they possess alike or in common, the term interest is applied both to the group so united and to the cause which unites them." He has also given us a valuable, though perhaps overly fine, distinction between interest and pressure group, by noting that to bring political, economic or social pressure to bear on government is not *inherent* in the concept of an interest group, whereas it is the defining function of a pressure group.[12]

Such groupings, broadly defined as interests, were (and still are) strategic units in British politics. Yet a further refinement is necessary, for in the eighteenth century—in the colonies as well as in England—there were both local, familiar, personal, and parliamentary connections, called interests, as well as broader regional, national, and imperial groupings also referred to in this way.[13] The former type was inextricably part of and usually subsumed by *one* of the latter, known as the landed interest. Our concern will be predominantly with the larger groupings, for while they were simultaneously less ephemeral and greater determinants of national and foreign policy, they have received little sustained notice from historians.

Even these interest groups, however, were far from similar in purpose, function, and importance. The Bank of England, the iron manufacturers, and the Protestant Dissenting Deputies were as dissimilar as the National Education Association, General Motors, and the National Rifle Association. Yet they all participated in the same political system, buying influence and maintaining skeletal organizations to sustain their concerns. In

---

[12] "Interests," and "Pressure Groups," *Encyclopedia of the Social Sciences* (New York, 1930-35). For a survey of definitions, see Roy C. Macridis, "Interest Groups in Comparative Analysis," *The Journal of Politics*, XXIII (1961), 27 ff.

[13] Beer, *British Politics*, p. 18; J. Steven Watson, *The Reign of George III, 1760-1815* (Oxford, 1960), pp. 55-56. For electoral interests in eighteenth-century Virginia, see Charles S. Sydnor, *American Revolutionaries in the Making: Political Practices in Washington's Virginia* (New York, 1965), pp. 45, 71; for interest-group politics in eighteenth-century New York, see Carl L. Becker, *The History of Political Parties in the Province of New York, 1760-1776* (Madison, Wis., 1909), pp. 11-15.

the eighteenth century, moreover, the vague distinction between public and private sectors—especially in financial matters and parliamentary acts—in addition to the nonrepresentation in Parliament of many elements in Georgian society—especially urban areas—tended to increase the number and activity of the interest groups. Even the administrative structure of government, suffering from departmentalism, was characterized by the presence of a Treasury interest, a Naval interest, a Post Office interest, and others that not only fought among themselves but competed with private interest groups virtually as equals![14] Understandably then, as a contributor wrote in the *Gentleman's Magazine*, "to recite the different struggles between these contending interests would require a volume."[15]

In examining and generalizing about these groups,[16] it is necessary to distinguish between mere *influence* and real political *power*, between mere access and the ability to achieve desired results. It is also important to note that groups were by no means monolithic—at least not consistently. The mercantile interest comprised a variety of dissimilar components, some of which, for example, thrived on political stability, while others did not.[17] Planters and merchants known as the West Indian interest did not always share common objectives, especially regarding

---

[14] Namier, *Structure of Politics*, pp. 363, 382; Ian R. Christie, "Economical Reform and 'the Influence of the Crown'; 1780," *Cambridge Historical Journal*, XII (1956), 150, 153; Daniel A. Baugh, *British Naval Administration in the Age of Walpole* (Princeton, 1965), pp. 19-21; Kustaa Hautala, *European and American Tar in the English Market During the Eighteenth and Early Nineteenth Centuries, Annales Academiae Scientiarum Fennicae*, CXXX (Helsinki, 1963), 51-54, 62, 86; Namier and Brooke, *The History of Parliament: The House of Commons, 1754-1790*, I, 138. For a discussion of the tendency of branches of government to behave like interest groups, see Joseph G. La Palombara, *Interest Groups in Italian Politics* (Princeton, 1964), p. 7.

[15] *Gentleman's Magazine*, XXXVI (May, 1766), 230.

[16] Generalizations throughout these chapters are based upon an examination of more than fifty interest groups. The reader will note that they are not all economic, but include religious, social, political, organized and informal groups.

[17] Plumb, "The Mercantile Interest: the Rise of the British Merchant After 1689," *History Today*, V (1955), 762-67.

monopoly prices and the direct trade to Europe.[18] The landed interest included both aristocracy and gentry, country gentlemen and larger farmers whose aims did not always coincide.[19] The East India Company's internal divisiveness was notorious.[20] Iron merchants and shippers often differed with forge owners[21]; the City of London's moneyed interest was not consistently a harmonious whole,[22] nor were the clothing and textile interests.[23] Moreover there were times and circumstances when an interest was a greater force in politics when internally divided than when cohesive and tranquil. The East India interest's role in the famous election of 1701 provides a case in point.[24] For much of the colonial period the North American interest lacked the singularity suggested by its name. While Pennsylvania's proprietors often had strong influence with the crown, Connecticut's influence was as negligible as that of any overseas dependency, and the two colonies occasionally matched wits and tested their relative strength in London.[25]

Nevertheless most of these aggregations enjoyed considerable stability and cohesion through long stretches of the eighteenth century, and at such times they were forceful and influential. One should not, however, naïvely regard them as fully discrete entities, for their memberships commonly

[18] Eric Williams, *Capitalism and Slavery* (Chapel Hill, N. C., 1944), chap. 4, esp. pp. 92-94.

[19] J. D. Chambers and G. E. Mingay, *The Agricultural Revolution, 1750-1880* (London, 1966), p. 121; Baugh, *British Naval Administration*, pp. 15-16.

[20] Namier and Brooke, *The History of Parliament: The House of Commons, 1754-1790*, I, 150.

[21] Arthur C. Bining, *British Regulation of the Colonial Iron Industry* (Philadelphia, 1933), p. 57.

[22] Marshall, *Eighteenth Century England*, p. 167.

[23] H. F. Kearney, "The Political Background to English Mercantilism, 1695-1700," *Economic History Review*, 2nd ser., XI (1959), 485.

[24] Robert Walcott, "The East India Interest in the General Election of 1700-1701," *English Historical Review*, LXXI (1956), 223-39.

[25] *The Susquehannah Company Papers*. Julian P. Boyd, ed., *Memorial Publications of the Wyoming Historical and Genealogical Society* (Wilkes-Barre, Pa., 1930-33), I, introduction.

overlapped and interlocked with governmental personnel as well as with each other. Many individuals among landed groups were greatly involved in the woolen industry, which led to alliances with textile manufacturers as against trading and commercial interests.[26] Yet the interests' identities were sufficiently distinct to be meaningful for contemporaries, who singled out and discussed one or another among them in responding to the dynamics of public life. Unlike a party or faction, the interests were not themselves prepared to undertake governmental responsibility. But their configuration and interaction provides a continuum, leading to and including the state and its policy-making organs.[27] These phenomena deserve close scrutiny, for their history, taken together, adds a broader dimension to our knowledge of Georgian Britain and its imperial possessions. Not surprisingly, that history seems to divide into periods punctuated by the great treaties rather than by the deaths and accessions of monarchs. The years 1696, 1713, 1748, 1763, and 1783 provide a convenient, if arbitrary, chronological structure upon which to develop our analysis.

THE POLITICS OF INTEREST BEFORE 1660

Interest groups were active, of course, long before the restoration of Charles II in 1660. Before industrialism the early growth of capitalism depended heavily upon luxury trades and government contracts. These very factors were also responsible for the creation of competitive private interests.[28] During the sixteenth century, many private bills were promoted in Parliament by boroughs, crafts, and companies, often

---

26 Williams, *Capitalism and Slavery*, pp. 92-93; Gerrit P. Judd, IV, *Members of Parliament, 1734-1832* (New Haven, 1955), p. 66; George Louis Beer, *British Colonial Policy, 1754-1765* (New York, 1907), p. 139.

27 Macridis, "Interest Groups in Comparative Analysis," p. 33; see also W. J. M. Mackenzie, "Pressure Groups in British Government," *British Journal of Sociology*, VI (1955), 133-48; "Pressure Groups: the 'Conceptual Framework,'" *Political Studies*, III (1955), 247-55.

28 See Namier's discussion of Werner Sombart's work in *The Structure of Politics*, p. 45.

through intensive lobbying. The City of London was particularly well-organized and from the fifteenth century had maintained a handsomely paid agent to look after its interests. Citizens were not to press any bill without the knowledge and consent of the Lord Mayor and Aldermen. London's four M.P.'s spearheaded this lobby in Parliament.[29]

All of these interest groups, as J. H. Hexter has observed, "and many, many more, separately and in coalitions of varying density and dimension created the actual economic conflicts of the early modern era." Later, in the eighteenth century, they would be responsible for major political conflicts as well. In Tudor England, however, and even through the mid-seventeenth century, these interests for the most part were subordinate to the state and its policy-making bodies.[30] Exponents of natural law theory agreed that subjection of local communities and corporate groups to state sovereignty distinguished them clearly from the state itself. In Hobbes' social schema, private associations derived their authority from the state, rather than from the community or its components. Hence, many in the seventeenth century trusted that governmental servants would not permit policy to be dominated by vested commercial interests, however strategic their importance.[31]

In part the Stuart governments' ability to control interest groups depended upon their competitive divisiveness. There

---

[29] J. E. Neale, *The Elizabethan House of Commons* (New Haven, 1950), pp. 383-87.

[30] *Reappraisals in History* (London, 1961), p. 193. P. J. Bowden, *The Wool Trade in Tudor and Stuart England* (London, 1962); Barry E. Supple, *Commercial Crisis and Change in England, 1600-1642* (Cambridge, Eng., 1959); S. T. Bindoff, "The Making of the Statute of Artificers," in S. T. Bindoff *et al.* eds., *Elizabethan Government and Society* (London, 1961), pp. 56-94. *Cf.* the argument of L. A. Clarkson, "English Economic Policy in the Sixteenth and Seventeenth Centuries: the Case of the Leather Industry," *Bulletin of the Institute of Historical Research,* XXXVIII (1965), 162.

[31] Otto Gierke, *Natural Law and the Theory of Society, 1500 to 1800* (Cambridge, Eng., 1934), I, 62, 81; Charles Wilson, *England's Apprenticeship, 1603-1763* (New York, 1965), part ii, *passim.*

were, for example, diverse and rival coal interests in seventeenth-century England. Owners of collieries near the coast, consumers, and middlemen could not agree and fought over what should be state policy.[32] In 1631, to cite another example, Charles I granted a monopoly to a group intending to manufacture soap by a new process from British materials exclusively. The other soap-makers were enraged, and their dispute rapidly acquired the dignity of an affair of state. Samuel R. Gardiner's amusing account of the result is worth quoting.

> The Council charged the soap-makers with suborning persons to spread false rumours to the disparagement of the Company's soap, and ordered the Attorney-General to commence a prosecution in the Star Chamber of some of their number who persisted in carrying on the manufacture without submitting to the Company's test. In order to meet the rumour by other means than prosecution, the Council directed that the new soap should be submitted to an impartial tribunal. The Lord Mayor, the Lieutenant of the Tower, together with sundry aldermen and men of note, were formed into a court of inquiry. When the court assembled, two washerwomen were introduced, to one of whom was handed a piece of the Company's soap, whilst the other was supplied with soap procured elsewhere. Tubs were brought in and a bundle of dirty clothes. When each washerwoman had done her best, the court pronounced that the clothes washed with the Company's soap "were as white and sweeter than" those which had been operated on by the production of the independent manufacturers. To add weight to this decision a declaration in its support from more than eighty persons of various ranks, peeresses and laundresses being included, was circulated with it.[33]

Clearly, the crown and Privy Council were in control; they could create monopolies and challenge interlopers. In establishing new corporations, Charles I, or those who acted in his

---

[32] John U. Nef, *The Rise of the British Coal Industry* (London, 1932), II, 209.
[33] Samuel R. Gardiner, *History of England from the Accession of James I to the Outbreak of the Civil War, 1603-1642* (London, 1884), VIII, 71-74, 282-87.

name, were often guided by considerations of public benefit. When the government interfered with aspects of domestic trade, it did so on the assumption that the King had a responsibility to see that his subjects were provided with articles of good quality, whether salt, wine, or soap.

Even so, it was clear by the eve of the Civil War in 1640 that interest groups were gaining in strength and political significance. The Corporation of Brickmakers was established in London in 1636. A year later the Corporation of Soapmakers was completely altered. The new group used its monopoly powerfully and exclusively. It applied constantly to the Privy Council for assistance in suppressing unauthorized manufacturers, and the Council usually complied. Opposition to crown attempts to extend its authority over the expanding coal trade came from members of the coal industry with increasing vehemence. Parliamentary hostility to particular patents was initiated by private traders. The same traders were responsible for efforts by municipal governments (which usually represented wealthy town merchants) to extend their own powers to include the need for regulation created by expansion of new industries. By the 1650's powerful coal-trading interests were very much in evidence.[34]

Throughout the seventeenth century the pressure of commercial interests on government grew, regardless of the current form of government. In the Commission of 1622, merchants such as Thomas Mun and government servants such as Lionel Cranfield worked together; both assumed that what was good for the merchant community was good for the nation at large. Before the Navigation Act of 1651 took shape—in many ways it was the first comprehensive piece of English mercantile legislation—merchants of the great companies showered the Council of State with petitions pleading their particular views. This Act, as well as its successors of the early Restoration years, did not represent a victory for any single group, however. It

---

[34] Nef, *British Coal Industry*, II, 240, 300, 323.

involved a compromise as government officials sought to reconcile the desires of the companies with those of the state.[35]

Kings and governments envisioned larger revenues and a
more prosperous—consequently tranquil—people to govern.
For merchants and their interests the State would provide assistance and protection. In short, in the halcyon days of mercantilism, there existed a working partnership in political economy.
Trading to remote places required aid from royal embassies
and the backing of government prestige. To sail through European and Asiatic waters, merchant ships needed convoys or
armed protection against privateers or belligerents. Immature
domestic industries needed bounties, subsidies, and incentives to
lure skilled foreigners to England. For all these reasons, then,
commercial interests sought state aid, "and saw in it the highest
embodiment of that corporate form of organisation to which
the traditions of gild and company had accustomed them."[36]

How, we may now ask, and where did colonies fit into this
frame of reference? Even more, how would colonies fare in
the fiercely competitive politics of mercantilism? The mercantilist practitioner wanted a monopoly of trade for the realm,
which meant England, Wales, and Berwick-upon-Tweed. He
would, therefore, exclude from this monopoly Ireland, Scotland (until 1707), and the colonies, except insofar as they
might profit incidentally from its indirect advantages. Colonies
must supplement, rather than compete with, the economy of
the mother state. To permit colonies to control their own economic life meant losing all the advantages inherent in possessing
colonies. By the eighteenth century many Britons believed that
colonial commercial interests were "using" British merchants
to further their own ends, and they very bitterly resented such
breaches of the colonial obligation.[37]

---

[35] J. E. Farnell, "The Navigation Act of 1651, the First Dutch War and
the London Merchant Community," *Economic History Review*, 2nd ser.,
XVI (1964), 439-54.

[36] Wilson, *Mercantilism*, pp. 18-19.

[37] Charles M. Andrews, *The Colonial Background of the American
Revolution* (New Haven, 1924), pp. 93-94.

During the first few decades of English overseas expansion, especially from 1607 to 1637, colonial concerns had been looked after in London with some care. In consequence, the English had gained several footholds in North America. After 1649, however, the City of London's financial interests became the predominant commercial voice in government circles. Not merely investors who had constituted the great chartered companies, they included individual merchants in unincorporated or interloping trades. Never before had these men been so numerous or influential. Under the first Stuarts, James and Charles, there had been a strong court interest in commercial and colonial affairs; but the turbulent events of the 1640's changed all that. Holders of proprietary colonial grants and trading monopolies, farmers of the customs, and stockholders in certain chartered companies, such as those for the Amazon and Guiana, were now of necessity subdued. Political strength rested with men hostile to colonial proprietorships and chartered companies, such as the East India and African, despite the fact that these had derived much of their earlier support from City financial interests. Where Stuart rule had been partial to particular monopolies, Commonwealth rule leaned more toward national monopolies. Instead of favoring some Englishmen at the expense of others, all Englishmen—at least all those within the realm—would now be favored over foreigners within the English sphere, especially the despised Dutch. Within a decade the position of American colonists in the imperial politics of mercantilism would again shift, ever so gradually, with profound results.[38]

---

[38] J. A. Williamson, "The Beginnings of an Imperial Policy, 1649-1660," in J. Holland Rose et al. eds., *The Cambridge History of the British Empire* (Cambridge, Eng., 1929), p. 214.

CHAPTER 2

INTERESTS IN EQUILIBRIUM, 1660-1696

RESTORATION FOR CAROLINE

Stuart statesmen regarded the welfare of the kingdom as their greatest responsibility. Their search for national improvement and stability convinced them of the need for subordinating the interests of individuals to those of the realm. Monopolies for the common weal were all-important, then, to prevent all others from profiting at England's expense. After 1660 trade and commerce became, as never before, matters of immediate governmental concern. In consequence mercantilist thinking gained even greater prominence. More than ever England's success and security seemed to lie in developing her foreign trade. During the reign of Charles II, however, a shift in thinking occurred. Gold and silver bullion were now less urgently thought of as commodities to be hoarded. What the Restoration mercantilists most wanted was a healthy margin of profit: protection against emergencies. Dutch, French, Italian, Danish, and German competition threatened England's European markets. Pamphleteers writing on matters of political economy, therefore, were gloomy and repetitiously fretful as they probed the causes of a commercial decay more imagined than real.[1]

---

[1] Ralph Davis, "English Foreign Trade, 1660-1700," *Economic History Review*, 2nd ser., VII (1954), 150-66.

They saw numerous causes and had numerous remedies. Their differences are perhaps more striking than their points of agreement. Yet their divisions into groups and factions were not extraordinary. Caroline England was divided generally into hostile groups and political factions. Indeed one of the loudest complaints of mercantile pamphleteers was that Parliament neglected the merchants' welfare and allowed factional and group loyalties to shape policy decisions. Mercantile spokesmen regarded the condition of foreign trade as a reflection of domestic affairs. They consequently condemned political manipulation, commercial speculation, and party quarreling as bad for business. They piously frowned on rebellion, war, preparation for war, and stock-jobbing, which thrived even in times of war.

A common denominator uniting mercantilists was their constant concern with unemployment and the working classes. Not particularly charitable souls, mercantilists simply wanted the lower orders of society to be efficient factors of production. They also agreed that colonial plantations were subordinate dependencies, suitable as sources of raw materials and markets for finished products of mother England. Ireland, perhaps because of proximity, was regarded by many as the most dangerous rival. Throughout our period her commercial independence was held in check, partly by the English Parliament and partly by her own. Ireland was permitted an independent linen industry in 1704 in order to support Protestant interests in the North, where flax-growing and linen-weaving had become major activities. Exports from northern Ireland to the colonies were modest and therefore had little effect upon crown revenues. After 1668 the Irish could send no cattle to England and were prohibited from competing with England's foremost staple, wool, either by raising the raw material or transforming it into fabrics. Not surprisingly, such policies aroused bitter discontent among the Irish and the numerous English living in Ireland.

The New World colonies, 3,000 slow miles away, were treated like Ireland—in principle. Actually, Americans had a somewhat easier time of it. The remote plantations were regarded as agricultural areas or tenancies, important to England as farming lands, outposts of trade, and sources of wealth. During the seventeenth century, several private colonies—corporate and proprietary—came under crown control, thereby joining the more numerous royal colonies. They were potential sources of profit whose trade should be restricted to the mother country. Otherwise, as one author put it, "there could be no reason for their establishment."[2]

Early in the seventeenth century, as we have seen, English authorities committed themselves to the belief that a nation should monopolize the trade of its plantations. Colonies as national assets appear early in mercantile literature. Yet neither the government nor the most prominent merchants seem to have taken the plantations or their trade very seriously at first. England's improvement at home was the most urgent thought. Colonies were very distant settlements of dubious value, ignored or misunderstood by many mercantilists. During the first two-thirds of the seventeenth century, Englishmen were more concerned with the East India trade and trade with France. Tangier, the fisheries, naturalization, rivalry with Holland, domestic poverty and the decay of trade were all more urgently felt issues in England than the nature and role of colonies in the imperial setup. When they were discussed at all in major works before the 1670's, it was only in connection with tobacco and sugar imports from Virginia and the West Indies.[3]

---

[2] Quoted in Charles M. Andrews, *The Colonial Period of American History* (New Haven, 1934-38), IV, 335.

[3] J. F. Rees, "Mercantilism and the Colonies," in J. Holland Rose *et al.*, eds., *The Cambridge History of the British Empire* (Cambridge, Eng., 1929), pp. 561-602. See also Margaret Priestley, "Anglo-French Trade and the 'Unfavourable Balance' Controversy, 1660-1685," *Economic History Review*, 2nd ser., IV (1951), 37-52.

In the 1660's and 1670's, however, colonizing in North America began again with renewed vigor, as Charles II rewarded his loyal courtiers with extravagant chunks of land which seemed endlessly expendable. Since Charles' government would not recognize legislation passed by Cromwell's Commonwealth, the Navigation Act of 1651 was a dead letter. From the very beginning of the Restoration, then, measures would have to be proclaimed in order to dominate and delineate the place of colonies in the developing empire.[4] Between 1660 and 1673 a strong beginning was made. By 1696 the Navigation "system," however unsystematic, was virtually complete.

On September 13, 1660, Parliament passed "An act for the Encouraging and Increasing of Shipping and Navigation." Though based upon the Act of 1651, its successor was considerably more far-reaching. Foreign vessels were absolutely excluded from participation in English colonial trade. Indeed, colonial trading ships must not only be English-owned, but also commanded by an English master and manned by a crew three-quarters English. Ships of foreign construction could be used in colonial trade only after English ownership had been certified before customs officials at home. Foreigners were strictly forbidden to "exercise the Trade or Occupation of Merchant or Factor" in the colonies. A new departure in the Act of 1660 was designed to safeguard certain colonial products regarded as particularly valuable for English self-sufficiency. Sugar, tobacco, wool, indigo, ginger, and other woods for dye colors could be shipped only to England or English territories.[5]

The colonial carrying trade had thus been legally confined to English shipping. Nevertheless the Act of 1660 did not

---

[4] P. L. Kaye, *English Colonial Administration Under Lord Clarendon, 1660-1667* (Baltimore, 1905).

[5] For this paragraph and the six following I have relied heavily upon Thomas C. Barrow, *The British Customs Service in Colonial America, 1660-1775* (Cambridge, Mass., 1967), chap. 1, and Lawrence A. Harper, *The English Navigation Laws: A Seventeenth-Century Experiment in Social Engineering* (New York, 1939), Part One.

necessarily channel all colonial commerce into England. Commodities other than those explicitly enumerated might be carried directly from the colonies to European countries; and foreign products might be imported to America without restriction, so long as they were all carried in English bottoms. Further legislation was needed if colonial economies were to function consistently with sound mercantile doctrine. Hence the Staple Act of 1663 was passed, providing that "No Commodity of the Growth, Production, or Manufacture of Europe, shall be imported into any . . . colony . . . but what shall be bona fide, and without Fraud, laden and shipped in England." Thereafter goods not specifically enumerated might still be taken from the colonies, in English ships, to foreign destinations. But any foreign products taken in exchange must first be brought to England, unloaded, and the proper duties paid, before the cargo could be reloaded for shipment to the plantations. This provision not only made England the focus of all trade; it enabled the penurious government of Charles II to increase its fiscal intake by collecting duties on foreign goods passing through England.

A few years of practical experience with these two acts revealed a serious defect in English conceptions of the nature of colonial commerce. Parliament and colonial planners in Whitehall had developed the Acts of 1660 and 1663 on the assumption that most colonial trade would be handled by shippers of English origin. They did not, and perhaps could not, anticipate the very rapid growth of intercolonial commerce, which could not be controlled as effectively as trade originating from English ports. By 1672 imperial authorities perceived that some enumerated products were covertly reaching foreign markets through the clandestine intricacies of intercolonial commerce. Consequently, still a third Navigation Act was passed in 1673, designed to prevent violations of acceptable mercantile orthodoxy. The Act declared that if any vessel arrived in the colonies to load enumerated goods, and "bond shall not be first given with sufficient Surety to bring the same to England," then duties must be paid even before the enumerated products might be loaded.

The Act of 1673, unlike its two predecessors, was not an altogether straightforward piece of legislation. The motives behind it were complex; its provisions were not clearly understood. The men responsible for it were particularly concerned that some colonists seemed to enjoy a tax advantage over their English competitors. The favored persons were not the southern and West Indian planters who actually raised the enumerated commodities, but the New England colonists who benefited especially from free importation. Consequently, the Act of 1673 was aimed particularly at them, the least valuable of all British possessions, it seemed. Indeed the northern colonies were potentially competitive with the mother country. They produced very few vitally needed raw materials and, as Professor Barrow has noted, "prospered only by adopting trade patterns which appeared detrimental to English interests."[6]

The Act of 1673, then, imposed duties which would indirectly provide some imperial revenue, and any additions to the depleted treasury of Charles II were most welcome. The intent of this third act was to remove from colonial competitors those tax-free benefits not available to Englishmen at home; to limit the intercolonial coasting trade, especially in those commodities desired in England; to reduce the shipment of enumerated goods sent directly to foreigners; to raise royal revenues by increasing supplies of such taxable imports as tobacco and sugar; and, generally, to tighten English control over colonial markets.

Once these three acts came into being, there remained the problem of enforcement. How could Whitehall and Parliament secure compliance 3,000 miles away in the wilderness of America? Even before 1673 appropriate steps were being taken. In addition to the use of bonds and registered shipping,

---

[6] Barrow, *The British Customs Service*, p. 9.

colonial governors were given explicit duties concerning enforcement of the Navigation Acts—all of these sanctions being continued and expanded throughout the colonial period. Because of obstacles to local enforcement, a colonial customs service was established. On October 26, 1671, an imperial agent was designated to collect the tobacco revenue in Virginia. He was the first royal customs officer appointed for the colonies. There would be many more in years to come. On November 27, 1673, the first comprehensive list of officers for the colonies was drafted. Five years later, with the appointment of Edward Randolph as collector, surveyor, and searcher of customs in New England, all English colonies in America came under the newly expanded customs service.

The Acts of Trade would function still more efficiently if evasions could be effectively controlled in those foreign countries where so many evasions in fact originated. Although customs officers could not be stationed in foreign ports, English diplomats and consular officials could report on illegal shipping and trading in their areas. Appropriate instructions were consequently sent to such personnel at necessary intervals. By the mid-1670's, therefore, a navigation "system" both sensible and workable seemed to have emerged. Regulations designed to control colonial trade in England's favor had been established by parliamentary acts. The English customs department, increasingly efficient at home, had been extended to the colonies. Both the Royal Navy and the diplomatic service were being used to assist in enforcement. Surely an auspicious beginning had been made for successful imperial administration.

By the 1680's, mercantile minds clearly grasped that plantations might be valuable assets on the commercial balance sheet. This became especially clear in 1685 when a heated debate took place over the increase of tobacco and sugar duties. By the 1690's a newer and still wider interest in colonies was aroused. In 1696 a writer petitioning Parliament insisted that "trade to the plantations," which was in an "irregular and disorderly state," was just as important as trade to the East

Indies.[7]   Other writers in 1696 regarded colonies as "our golden mines," hence all the more reason to impose order and regularity upon them. Those qualities were, in fact, theoretically achieved in 1696-1697 through passage of the last Navigation Act and subsequent administrative orders. The officious Edward Randolph, imperious administrators in London, and the powerful House of Lords combined to effect a new policy aimed at stricter and more centralized control over the colonies.[8]

As surveyor-general of customs in America since 1691, Randolph had run the frustrating gauntlet of resistance to the Navigation Acts. Goods were smuggled, customs collectors were dishonest, local juries would not bring in convictions against local personalities, and colonial governors were indifferent if not actually opposed to strict enforcement. Randolph returned to England in the summer of 1695 and promptly submitted to the Customs House a searing indictment of disfunction in the navigation system. In a few months' time, when Parliament inquired into the state of the nation, Randolph's criticisms and recommendations became topics of national debate. Parliament made such an inquiry because pressures of war with France, widespread illegal trade, and the expectation that a group of Scottish and English entrepreneurs would organize a trading company at Darien, on the isthmus between North and South America, all focused urgent attention upon the Empire in the winter of 1695-1696.[9]

Early in December representatives of various English trading companies, the Customs House, and English subscribers to the

[7] "The Irregular and Disorderly State of the Plantation-Trade," *Annual Report of the American Historical Association for the Year 1892* (Washington, 1893), p. 36.

[8] See Michael G. Hall, *Edward Randolph and the American Colonies, 1676-1703* (Chapel Hill, N.C. 1960); Gertrude Ann Jacobsen, *William Blathwayt: A Late Seventeenth Century English Administrator* (New Haven, 1932).

[9] Michael G. Hall, "The House of Lords, Edward Randolph, and the Navigation Act of 1696," *William and Mary Quarterly*, 3rd ser., XIV (1957), 494-515.

Darien Company were examined by the House of Lords. After several hearings the Lords sought from the customs commissioners a written statement of devices by which Scottish schemes in America might be circumvented. Several months of hearings and politicking ensued, leading in April to passage by both houses of the last Navigation Act. Essentially a regulatory measure aimed at tightening the apparatus of colonial administration, it clarified ambiguities in earlier acts, reinforced the responsibility of colonial governors for enforcement, and arranged for new penalties. Other provisions, by implication, went quite beyond the intent of Restoration legislation by actually altering the colonies' constitutional relationship with the crown. The most striking implicit innovation involved establishment in the colonies of vice-admiralty courts with jurisdiction over penal clauses in the Navigation Acts. Ordinarily vice-admiralty courts had jurisdiction over prizes and piracy, but not over Navigation Acts. But because colonies seemed to present special problems, special measures were needed to meet them. Hence, extraordinary jurisdiction was granted to admiralty courts in America.

A month later still another organizational change was made, one which would complete the creation of colonial administrative machinery and give it permanent form for generations to come. In May, 1696, the Board of Trade replaced the Committee for Trade and Plantations which had supervised colonial affairs since 1675.[10] The most intricate political maneuvering preceded the emergence of the new board as crown and Parliament pushed and shoved in search of control over the strategic institution. In years to come the Board would often

10 See Charles M. Andrews, *British Committees, Commissions, and Councils of Trade and Plantations, 1622-1675* (Baltimore, 1908); Ralph P. Bieber, "The British Plantation Councils of 1670-4," *English Historical Review*, XL (1925), 93-106; Ralph P. Bieber, *Lords of Trade and Plantations, 1675-1696* (Allentown, Pa., 1919); R. M. Lees, "Parliament and the Proposal for a Council of Trade, 1695-96," *English Historical Review*, LIV (1939), 38-66; and Peter Laslett, "John Locke, the Great Recoinage, and the Origins of the Board of Trade: 1695-1698," *William and Mary Quarterly*, 3rd ser., XIV (1957), 370-402.

be politically divided between advocates of strict colonial control, such as William Blathwayt, and more enlightened intellectuals such as John Locke, sensitive to colonial needs and aspirations.[11] By the spring of 1697 the House of Lords had made the Navigation Act of 1696—the so-called Act for Preventing Frauds—into a law of major constitutional importance, especially in undermining the authority of overly-autonomous colonies. By the close of the seventeenth century, the institutional potential for imperial conflict existed.

In summary, the Act of 1651, which aimed at removing Dutch merchants and shipmasters from the import trade into England, was as shortlived as the Commonwealth. Before politicians or colonial administrators had any way of measuring its effect, it was supplanted by new acts in 1660, 1663, and 1673. Thereafter Anglo-American trade was enclosed and protected by English vessels. Earlier attempts to prevent the drain of bullion by directly banning its export were now largely abandoned. Englishmen were more concerned with developing the volume and value of exports, limiting the volume and value of imports, eliminating unnecessary imports in Dutch and foreign shipping, and gaining as much income as possible through the carrying trade. After more than forty years the mercantile proposals of Thomas Mun and his associates had become a reality.[12]

Yet the apogee of English mercantilism and colonial control was not achieved without intense political turmoil. The reigns of Charles II, James II, and William III were notable for significant shifts in the organization of political society. Parties, factions, and especially diverse economic interests helped to create crises and in turn were heavily affected by those crises. We must next consider the structure and nature of interest politics during the last third of the seventeenth century.

---

[11] Michael G. Kammen, "Virginia at the Close of the Seventeenth Century: an Appraisal by James Blair and John Locke," *Virginia Magazine of History and Biography*, LXXIV (1966), 141-53.

[12] Charles Wilson, *Mercantilism* (London, 1958), pp. 16-17.

THE POLITICS OF INTEREST, 1660-1696

The revival of English commerce after 1660 was much favored by Charles II and his brother, the Duke of York. Great trading companies requested and received new charters with augmented grants of power to facilitate their growing trade. The East India Company, for example, obtained a new charter including judicial powers, and control over Bombay and St. Helena. The Turkey Company also received a new charter, as did the African Company (canceled because of debts, and regranted in 1672). During the 1660's the Council of Trade debated the plight of the English fishing industry and promptly authorized establishment of the Company of the Royal Fishery of Great Britain and Ireland. In 1670 a new company was chartered for trading purposes in the Hudson's Bay region. Charles II generously granted the Hudson's Bay Company an enormous territory to which his claim was highly dubious.[13]

Given extensive powers, some companies became quite ruthless. The East India Company set up courts at Bombay and St. Helena that could be extraordinarily harsh. These trading titans were also exceedingly influential in shaping the course of English foreign policy. The Royal African and East India Companies were partially responsible for causing the second Anglo-Dutch war (1672-1674); the Hudson's Bay Company's grievances against the French were important ingredients in Anglo-French friction later in the century. The French claimed prior rights in regions allotted to the Company, and tried to oust it through terrorist tactics. The Company in turn complained to the government and sought protection. William III made these grievances a major justification for war with France, and made the Hudson's Bay region an objective in both war-making and peace-making.[14]

[13] Charles Wilson, *Profit and Power, A Study of England and the Dutch Wars* (London, 1957), chaps. 7-8.

[14] See Margaret Priestley, "London Merchants and Opposition Politics in Charles II's Reign," *Bulletin of the Institute of Historical Research*, XXIX (1956), 205-19.

There was, nevertheless, considerable opposition to the companies at home, from private traders and smaller economic groups. The African Company was almost ruined in the slave trade by interlopers and pirates. The East India Company suffered similar problems. The famous case of *Thomas Skinner* v. *the East India Company* led to a bitter fight within Parliament over the Company's privileges and jurisdictions and lingered on for a quarter-century. Many minor companies had to struggle in order to evade the might of the great monopolies. The Canary Company, for example, was shortlived because of powerful opposition and corruption in obtaining its charter. Even so, Charles II favored the Canary Company until Parliament virtually forced the recall of its charter. His general partiality to the companies is easily understood. They made loans and gave him gifts. Charles and James both were stockholders in several such enterprises. Finally, trade in tea, spices, bullion, saltpeter, and slaves meant wealth for the realm, powder for the military, and slaves for colonial planters.

The Glorious Revolution of 1688-89 altered the constitutional relationship between crown and commercial companies. Royal prerogative was reduced and Parliament became a greater power in government than before. Thereafter the companies could no longer beseech only the King to grant them a charter of exclusive monopoly. They had to look to Parliament for legitimacy, and many had difficulty in winning the necessary sanctions. In 1693, for example, the East India Company forfeited its charter because of failure to pay a tax when it fell due. Significantly, the Company's political orientation at that time was Tory, while Whigs dominated Parliament. Moreover, a well-organized group of interlopers was determined to destroy the Company. Some of these men had once been members of the East India Company, but had been forced out. In order to defeat them by winning over Parliament, Sir Josiah Child, an influential merchant-politician, resorted to bribery in high places to get the charter renewed and an act of Parliament sanctioning the monopoly. He succeeded, but exposure of the scandal discredited the Company. Immediately interlopers tried to take advantage of the Company's weakened position by having it condemned in Parliament. In 1698 Parliament incorporated a rival East India Company which advanced the government an extraordinary sum of £2,000,000. The East India trade was now divided by bitter rivalry. The only way to consolidate English power in the Far East was through unification, a political decision made at the highest reaches of government. In 1702 a preliminary agreement was achieved, and formalized in 1709. The United East India Company was ready to begin laying the foundation of the British Empire in India.[15]

The Hudson's Bay Company had no difficulty gaining parliamentary sanction for its charter in 1690, chiefly because its complaints involved the hated French and its monopoly had not become so heavy-handed as those of other companies. Nevertheless London feltmakers complained that the Company sold furs illegally, and its monopoly was opposed as a threat to the "Russia trade" in furs. There was strong political competition throughout this period between large furriers and skinners, and small hatters or felters.[16] The trade of the Hamburg Company began in 1688, but did not flourish. The Greenland and Fishery Companies were revived after the Revolution, but had little influence then on governmental policies. The Levant Company, however, did require governmental attention because of its rivalry with the East India Company in exporting goods to the East. The Levant Company contended that its competitor poached upon its territory, especially in Persia.

The Royal African Company had suffered continually at the hands of both interlopers and colonial planters. These less

---

[15] Ancil N. Payne, *The Relation of the English Commercial Companies to the Government, 1660-1715* (Urbana, Ill., 1930).

[16] E. E. Rich, "Russia and the Colonial Fur Trade," *Economic History Review*, 2nd ser., VII (1955), 319, 323.

organized but intensely active groups complained repeatedly to the government, more than ever after 1688, and more successfully because the Company no longer had the King's immediate backing. The crown had in fact lost its power to grant an exclusive monopoly to a trading company. Parliament stepped in, and in 1698 opened the African trade to private traders who would pay the Company a ten percent cut, to be applied to the maintenance of forts in Africa. For nearly fifty years thereafter, the Royal African Company would have little influence on government policy.

The "politics of interest" during the final third of the seventeenth century, then, underwent significant changes because of political and constitutional crises, but also because of alterations in England's position in international trade. In the decade or so following the Anglo-Dutch War of 1664-1667, a shift occurred in British political society, particularly its component interest groups. Although the war failed to gain for the English access to the spice trade of the East Indies, it did lead to establishment of fuller English hegemony over a whole complex network of Atlantic trades, including tobacco, sugar, fur, slaves, and codfish. The increased permeation of imperial society by commercial value and creation of a structure of trade regulation, mentioned earlier, were accompanied by the proliferation of new or expanded interest groups. Almost simultaneously the Royal African, Royal Fishery, and Hudson's Bay Companies appeared (1670-1672). A large-scale importation of Negroes from West Africa soon accompanied the tobacco boom, which in turn led to the appearance of two groups: the Russian Tobacco Company and the Virginia Merchants of London. A closely related phenomenon was the long-term growth of Liverpool, beginning late in the 1660's. The sugar refining industry, developed in London and Bristol since 1544 and 1612, took hold in Glasgow after 1667. The West India merchants originated in the 1670's as London commission agents. By the close of the decade, Scotland's interest in colonial trade revived generally, and led to the formation of new groups with broader economic and social bases there.[17]

While the presence and role of such groups increased, attitudes toward them were also changing. A recurrent question of the seventeenth century, appearing again and again in instructions to councils of trade, asked "whether it be necessary to give way to a more open and free trade than that of companies and societies?"[18] In the 1670's a rather inconsistent response emerged. Parliament's hostility toward monopolies seemed to fall heavily on companies engaged in trade to Europe and the East, leaving the new trans-Atlantic interests to their preferred positions.[19] Debate over monopolies continued with some feeling through the last two decades of the century; but regardless of whether the basic units of economic activity were to be monolithic or fragmented, the very fact of debate testified to the vigorous commercial organization of society.[20]

The underpinnings of this debate were less intellectual or ideological than ruthlessly practical. There were simply massive power struggles between rival groups of merchants competing for control of foreign trade. Significantly, however, whenever England's political situation in European affairs became critical, narrow group interests had to stand aside.[21] Clearly, Daniel Defoe's *Essay Upon Projects*, written earlier but published in 1697, was a tract for its times, which the

---

[17] D. A. Farnie, "The Commercial Empire of the Atlantic, 1607-1783," *The Economic History Review*, 2nd ser., XV (1962), 206-11, 214; Andrews, *The Colonial Period*, IV, 114, 117, 153; Jacob M. Price, *The Tobacco Adventure to Russia, Transactions of the American Philosophical Society*, new series, LI, part 1 (Philadelphia, 1961), pp. 6-7, 22; E. Lipson, *The Economic History of England*, II, *The Age of Mercantilism* (6th ed.; London, 1956), chap. 2, for a discussion of the great companies.

[18] R. W. K. Hinton, *The Eastland Trade and the Common Weal in the Seventeenth Century* (Cambridge, Eng., 1959), p. vii.

[19] Christopher Hill, *The Century of Revolution, 1603-1714* (Edinburgh, 1961), pp. 213-15; one notable exception was the demise of the Bermuda Company in 1684.

[20] Philip W. Buck, *The Politics of Mercantilism* (New York, 1942), p. 124; John Collins, *Salt and Fishery* (London, 1682).

[21] Sven-Erik Åström, *From Cloth to Iron: the Anglo-Baltic Trade in the Late Seventeenth Century* (Helsingfors, 1963), pp. 185-86.

author called a "Projecting age." In trying to account for "such a multitude of Projectors more than usual," he stressed the impetus of war and the burgeoning of stock companies.[22] Between 1660 and 1685, only six trading companies were chartered by the state, as against thirteen in as many years after 1685.[23] When Daniel Coxe, physician to Charles II and later Queen Anne, became excited about land schemes in North America, he drew leaders of English society and government from every political persuasion into the venture. His New Mediterranean Sea Company scheme in 1686 was to use Lake Erie as an effective base from which to monopolize the Indian trade of Pennsylvania. Despite his influential connections the plan was abortive, but its ambitiousness and New World thrust were characteristic of Defoe's "Projecting age."[24]

During the reign of Charles II, interest groups whose attentions focused on North America were very active in London. These trans-Atlantic lobbies commonly comprised a marriage of convenience between two sorts of groups—for example Virginia tobacco planters and political leaders, and London merchant-adventurers trading to Virginia. Although they shared common political goals, they also found their particular interests in conflict from time to time. Significantly the London-based group was much more powerful, and had greater leverage. Even more important, however, the two groups working together could achieve notable gains.[25]

---

[22] The excesses associated with "projecting" were satirized by Swift in *Gulliver's Travels* through the Grand Academy of Lagado. Benjamin Franklin was much impressed with Defoe's *Essay*, and quoted it later in an age of interest politics undreamed-of even by Defoe.

[23] Cecil T. Carr, ed., *Select Charters of Trading Companies, A.D. 1530-1707* [*Publications of the Selden Society*, XXVIII] (London, 1913).

[24] Albright G. Zimmerman, "Daniel Coxe and the New Mediterranean Sea Company," *Pennsylvania Magazine of History and Biography*, LXXVI (1952), 86-96.

[25] Sister Joan de Lourdes Leonard, "Operation Checkmate: the Birth and Death of a Virginia Blueprint for Progress, 1660-1676," *William and Mary Quarterly*, 3rd ser., XXIV (1967), 45-46, 49, 53; Neville Williams, "The Tribulations of John Bland, Merchant: London, Seville, Jamestown, Tangier, 1643-1680," *Virginia Magazine of History and Biography*, LXXII (1964), pp. 19-29.

Lobbyists sent directly from the colonies at this time often found their task bitterly frustrating. Sir William Berkeley, Governor of Virginia, arrived in London in 1661 to seek revision of the Navigation Act of 1660, assistance for the Anglican church in Virginia, and financial aid for economic diversification in the colony. Late in 1662 Sir William sailed westward sadly with "nothing more than suggestions and admonitions as to the ways in which Virginia might help itself out of its own difficulties." He failed to gain revision, revenue, or royal assistance for the struggling church.[26] Virginia's weakness at the Restoration Court is almost as surprising as Connecticut's simultaneous success, for during the very same years John Winthrop, Jr., gained access to Lord Chancellor Clarendon and obtained more land for Connecticut as well as durable self-government under a royal charter. In the process he sealed the fate of New Haven's struggling colony and shaped the new Rhode Island charter as well, which would outlast even her neighbor's. The amiable Winthrop was a wily, if not ruthless, lobbyist. Finding that mercantilists and bureaucrats differed markedly from courtiers on how best to manage and develop the plantations in 1662-1663, he exploited their divisiveness with pecuniary pressure, personal presence, and influential connections.[27]

By the 1660's the permanent pattern of New England's economy had crystallized, and her merchants became prominent figures in a complex set of oceanic trade relationships. Within a decade their London counterparts were deeply suspicious of the New Englanders' growing interest in the Newfoundland trade, especially at a time when two groups of Englishmen were vying for control of the Newfoundland fishing industry. London merchants sought profits from transporting fish prepared by a permanent colony settled in Newfoundland, while

---

[26] Wesley Frank Craven, *The Colonies in Transition, 1660-1713* (New York, 1968), pp. 32-33, 39-43.

[27] Richard S. Dunn, *Puritans and Yankees: The Winthrop Dynasty of New England, 1630-1717* (Princeton, 1962), pp. 126-29, 131-34, 136-42.

West Country men hoped to discourage colonization in order to maintain their domination of the annual fishing fleets. Both groups felt threatened by New Englanders, whose trade with Newfoundland was perfectly consistent with both the letter and spirit of the new Navigation Acts.[28]

The New England mast trade, a large and complicated business, also involved two distinct groups whose interests might easily conflict: London entrepreneurs who contracted with the government, and New England merchants who actually exported timber. The first group consisted of powerful merchants with considerable amounts of available capital. "These contractors operated," as Bernard Bailyn has noted, "with all the arts of high-pressure negotiators, from cornering the supply to cultivating friendships with governmental officials like Pepys. Of the colonial merchants engaged in the American end of the business, the most successful were those with the best connections in London." Although a closely controlled monopoly of the mast trade and government contracts would have been highly desirable to the ambitious groups involved, such a condition was not possible in the three decades after 1660. "In England the rivalries among governmental and business cliques were too intense and the system of awarding contracts too susceptible to a variety of pressures to allow long-term monopolies." That would develop only at the very end of the century.[29]

By the later 1670's, New Englanders had clearly come to regard their needs and aspirations as a special interest separate from other competing groups in London. Governors such as Leverett of Massachusetts Bay saw as their peculiar responsibility the proper defense of "the Interest of New England." To achieve this end, both New England and Chesapeake colonies had begun to send paid lobbyists, called agents, to London to look after their affairs. At first such agents were

[28] Bernard Bailyn, *The New England Merchants in the Seventeenth Century* (Cambridge, Mass., 1955), pp. 86, 113, 130.
[29] *Ibid.*, pp. 133, 155-56.

sent on temporary missions to achieve particular ends at court and in Parliament. By 1690 more regular agencies had been established whereby lobbyists worked permanently in England to defend the interests of their employers.[30]

During a pivotal period in the reign of Charles II, such agents had to contend with the dominant English statesman concerned with colonial policy, Anthony Ashley Cooper, First Earl of Shaftesbury (1621-1683). This politically ambitious intellectual was personally involved in many of the schemes typical of Defoe's "Projecting age": the Iron and Steel Corporation, the Royal African Company, the Whalebone Company, the Mines Royal, the Carolinas, Bahamas and New Providence Island, Barbados and Hudson's Bay. He fully appreciated that "it was folly to neglect the advice or the interest of the merchants or of the producers." Yet he also believed that "where the merchant trades for a great deale of Profit the nation loses."[31]

In brief, Shaftesbury is symbolic of the later seventeenth century as an age of interests in equilibrium—among themselves and *vis-à-vis* government. The chartered companies of the Restoration attracted both the merchant classes and landed gentry, a social fact which helped keep the interests in balance. Shaftesbury's presidency of the Board of Trade during the 1670's was characterized by flexibility and a healthy aversion to dogma in colonial affairs. "It is Trade and Commerce alone that draweth store of wealth along with it, and that potency at sea by shipping which is not otherwise to be had." Nevertheless the commerce which could facilitate these benefits was "Commerce as an affair of State," which was "widely different from the mercantile part," and would often lead to policies apparently contradictory to private interests of merchants. The Lords of Trade, therefore, must be able to dis-

---

[30] Michael G. Kammen, *A Rope of Sand: the Colonial Agents, British Politics and the American Revolution* (Ithaca, N.Y., 1968), chap. 1.

[31] E. E. Rich, "The First Earl of Shaftesbury's Colonial Policy," *Transactions of the Royal Historical Society*, 5th ser., VII (London, 1957), 56, 60, 62.

tinguish the proper aims of the state from personal goals of private groups.[32]

The deepening imperial crisis of the 1680's elicited a flurry of special interest agitation by colonials in London. William Penn and Charles Calvert, third Lord Baltimore, competed in the Old World for land and power in the New. Penn had, as he put it, "great entrance and interest with the K[ing James II]," and won this first round in a protracted bout. But additional territory was procured at great cost, for Penn's connection with the Stuart despot would shortly cast him into sore distress.[33] Meanwhile Richard Wharton, Increase Mather, Sir William Phips and others, leaders secular and spiritual, sailed for London in 1687-1688 to seek a new charter for Massachusetts Bay and, not incidentally, healthy chunks of land for speculative citizens there. Their success in 1691 seemed to herald auspicious times ahead for American Whigs in New England and the Chesapeake too. Indeed, there were now influential men and factions in several colonies whose English connections gained for them power to circumvent colonial governors and even sap their authority.[34]

As William and Mary maneuvered for stability and settlement in the early 1690's, lobbying for and by North American colonies became a characteristic part of the political tableau in London. Fitz John Winthrop, grandson of John the founder and son of John, Jr., of Connecticut, came over in 1693 to defend his chartered colony against complaints and remained for four years to lobby on various issues. In the process he won the respect of the influential Earl of Bellomont and the Board of Trade. Although Fitz John had to accept new restrictions on his colony's privileges, he at least was able to confirm Connecticut's semi-autonomous position within the Empire. This was interest politics in equilibrium. In the process he ran head-on into agents from other colonies—two from New York

---

[32] *Ibid.*, pp. 61-62.

[33] Joseph E. Illick, *William Penn the Politician: His Relations with the English Government* (Ithaca, N.Y., 1965), pp. 65-67, 86, 88.

[34] Craven, *Colonies in Transition*, pp. 222, 234, 241, 245, 268.

with whom he battled over defense appropriations—and made friends with William Penn and Sir Henry Ashurst, resident agent of Massachusetts. By the close of 1696 Winthrop voiced to Connecticut his concern for all "the other proprietary governments, viz. Carolina, Pensilvania, the Jersyes, & Rhode Island . . . who are under one interest of liberty & priviledg with yourselves."[35] He foresaw clearly the subsequent emergence of a North American interest, still several generations away.

Meanwhile William Penn began shedding the leprous taint of past association with James II, and became a spokesman for proprietors and agents who represented private colonies in England. These men would insist, unavailingly, that their respective charters allowed them to establish their own admiralty jurisdictions. But as Penn's political friends returned to office in 1694, he would find success on other matters: his continuing conflict with the Calverts of Maryland, and the all-important return of his colony from royal control. Once again we find interest politics in equilibrium as Penn struggled with the balance wheel of his dilemma: how to satisfy both the demands of the home government and the desires of Pennsylvanians for autonomy.[36]

ECONOMIC THEORY AND IMPERIAL EQUILIBRIUM

During the final third of the seventeenth century, greater attention was paid to discussions of economic theory than ever before. Most writers of this period, as Max Beer has pointed out, "wrote with a conscious bias to defend or combat certain group or party interests, and they used as instruments the economic thoughts and formulae created in the past, either for or against those interests."[37] In the view of one, most trade laws

---

[35] Dunn, *Puritans and Yankees*, pp. 298, 302-04, 307-08, 311-14.

[36] Illick, *William Penn the Politician*, pp. viii, 123, 126, 128, 138-41, 145, 153, 169-70.

[37] Max Beer, *Early British Economics from the Thirteenth to the Middle of the Eighteenth Century* (London, 1938), p. 197.

that had appeared since the 1660's "were calculated rather for particular interest than public good; more to advance some tradesmen than the trade of the nation."[38] During this generation, social and economic groupings in British public life commonly came to be called "interests," and a congeries of opinions emerged on how best to regulate them for the public good while insuring that the regulations themselves were not molded by the groups.[39]

Although mercantilist doctrine stressed the importance of national economic interests, it also contained implicitly the potential disharmony between particular commercial groups, individual merchants, and classes on the one hand, and the welfare of the commonwealth as a whole, on the other. Thus, in theory at least, refusal to make concessions to particular interests was not tantamount to disregarding the national interest, as they conceived it. Nonetheless, there was a significant gap between theory and practice that widened as the seventeenth century drew to a close. The dispute among mercantilists over the status of monopolistic companies, for example, revealed quite plainly that "the mutual interests of organized groups, or of the recognized classes of society . . . were not so widely agreed upon as they cheerfully supposed."[40] Protracted conflict between the East India Company and the woolen manufacturers accentuated and dramatized this growing tension.[41]

Under mercantilism various private interests understandably regarded their own well-being as essential to that of the state, despite idealization of the state as something more than a mere

---

[38] [John Pollexfen], *Discourse of Trade, Coyn, and Paper Credit* (London, 1697), p. 149.

[39] *The Oxford English Dictionary* . . . (Oxford, 1933), V, 394; Buck, *Politics of Mercantilism*, p. 135; Jacob Viner, "English Theories of Foreign Trade Before Adam Smith," *Journal of Political Economy*, XXXVIII (1930), 436.

[40] Jacob Viner, "Power Versus Plenty as Objectives of Foreign Policy in the 17th and 18th Centuries," *World Politics*, I (1948), 19; Buck, *Politics of Mercantilism*, pp. 87, 173-74.

[41] Max Beer, *Early British Economics*, p. 238.

aggregation of private groups.[42] Moreover the burden of proof for any publicist engaged by an interest group came to be the assertion that his employers' prosperity was in no way incompatible with that of the landed interest, the largest, most amorphous, and most important of all interests during this era. Under the last Stuarts some contemporaries identified Tories with the landed interest and Whigs with the commercial, though writers of ephemeral and philosophical literature did their best to blur such distinctions, increasingly so under the first two Georges.[43] "There has been an attempt in ENGLAND," Hume wrote, "to divide the *landed* and *trading* part of the nation; but without success. The interests of these two bodies are not really distinct."[44]

The need for a council of trade was a staple idea of mercantilists, even though they could not readily agree on its proper composition. Disputes on this point became especially strong during the 1670's and 1680's, indicative of the intellectual ferment concerning the relative role of interest groups. Many assumed that such a body would be a board of merchants, though others, rather heretically, wanted merchants, manufacturers, *and* the landed interest represented. Sir Josiah Child assumed that only when merchants bought lands would they become of "the same common interest with most of their Countrymen." William Paterson devised an elaborate machinery in which both interest groups and classes would be represented in such a council: three from the high nobility, three from the estate of the barons, three from the boroughs, and three from the Indian and African companies.[45]

---

[42] Robert L. Schuyler, *The Fall of the Old Colonial System* (New York, 1945), p. 8.

[43] Archibald S. Foord, *His Majesty's Opposition, 1714-1830* (Oxford, 1964), p. 20; See L. W. Hanson, *Contemporary Printed Sources for British and Irish Economic History, 1701-1750* (Cambridge, Eng., 1963), nos. 2303, 2774, 3024, 4350, 5028.

[44] "Of Parties in General," *Essays Moral, Political, and Literary* (London, 1889), I, 130.

[45] Buck, *Politics of Mercantilism*, pp. 135-37; Viner, "English Theories of Foreign Trade," pp. 436-37.

The quest for cohesion among the great interests was hardly a futile one in these years, however, and in many areas the literature reflected reality. In the north country the great age of the gentry during the first half of the eighteenth century was made possible by profits derived earlier from trade, especially coal mining and related enterprises. The result was "a greater fusion of landed and merchant interest in these parts than elsewhere."[46] Because landed society dominated the House of Lords and controlled a large minority in the House of Commons, and because its influence locally was massive, all other interests were obliged to accommodate themselves accordingly or at least rationalize such an accommodation for political effect.[47] The essayists Addison and Steele noted this early in the century, and Hume a generation later. By mid-century, however, the effort to prove the compatibility of influential groups with the landed and national interests took on an air of unreality. The shrillness and earnestness of pamphleteers' pleas seemed to belie their conviction and the truth of their contentions. "Between the Landed and Trading Interest in this Kingdom there ever has been, and ever will be an inseparable Affinity," one wrote. "They mutually furnish each other with all the Conveniences of Life, and no real Preference can be given either to the one or to the other. It is demonstrably true, that it can never go ill with Trade but Land will fall nor ill with Land but Trade will feel it."[48] Perhaps George Coade believed what he said. Others among his contemporaries—defenders of the City of London, West Indian and African merchants, fisheries people, privateering ventur-

---

[46] L. B. Namier, *Personalities and Powers* (London, 1955), p. 85.

[47] G. E. Mingay, *English Landed Society in the Eighteenth Century* (London, 1963), pp. 111-15; G. P. Judd, *Members of Parliament, 1734-1782* (New Haven, 1955), chap. 9; Dorothy Marshall, *Eighteenth Century England* (London, 1962), p. 57.

[48] Paul W. Conner, *Poor Richard's Politicks. Benjamin Franklin and His New American Order* (New York, 1965), p. 121 ff.; George Coade, *A Letter to the Honourable Lords Commissioners of Trade and Plantations* (London, 1747), p. 21.

CHAPTER 3

THE AGE OF WALPOLE, 1696-1748

MERCANTILE POLICY AND MERCANTILE PRACTICE

From 1702 until 1713, during the international war which many feared would cost England her American colonies, a new consideration became prominent in mercantile thinking. Naval stores were added to tobacco and sugar as colonial staples profitable to England. Pitch, tar, turpentine, and hemp looked so promising as plantation commodities that they were placed on the enumerated list in 1705, and bounties were granted to encourage their production in three acts passed by Parliament between 1705 and 1729. During these same years a significant shift occurred in mercantilist thinking concerning the value of colonies to the mother country. Partially the change was due to the rapidly growing American population. Quickened immigration of Huguenots, Scots-Irish, and Germans after 1690 had a marked effect upon the expansion of colonial commerce, staples, and shipping.

The national debt increased fivefold between 1695 and 1713, causing mercantilists especially to seek ways to ease England's financial burdens, now at their highest in history. A solution seemed apparent to them through advancing foreign trade by extending credit, reducing duties, and transferring to landed

estates a larger share of current taxation. The landed gentry
disagreed, however, and a dispute arose between them and the
merchants over customs revenue, land taxes, and excises. Their
dispute would crest in 1733 with the explosive excise episode.
As early as 1717, however, mercantilists were arguing that the
landed classes should carry a greater weight of taxation, especially since they profited from trade successes. Nevertheless,
despite differences over taxation, all agreed that a nation heavily
in debt could best resolve its dilemma through increased foreign trade. Doing so in the past had helped England surmount
crises and fight expensive wars.[1]

The leading mercantilist writer of this generation was
William Wood, secretary to the commissioners of the customs.
His *Survey of Trade*, published in 1718, argued vigorously for
foreign trade as England's staff of life. During the last third of
the seventeenth century, Josiah Child and Charles Davenant
had discussed the colonies in their writings, but Wood first
treated the plantations in depth as part of a full analysis of the
imperial situation after 1713. He was a "compleat mercantilist,"
approving of the Navigation Acts, opposing commercial agreements with France, opposing monopolies for chartered groups
such as the East India Company and the Royal African Company, and insisting that colonial trade should be subordinated
to the needs of the realm.

Wood's new emphasis upon the role of colonies in redressing
the balance for England led him and others to a strategic reconsideration of the importance of the middle and New England
colonies. They had seemed potential menaces to Josiah Child's
generation. To Wood and others of Walpole's era, however,
the northern provinces were becoming important markets for
English manufactured goods, and even more important in fur-
nishing supplies to the southern and Caribbean colonies. After
1713 all colonial resources were regarded as important in con-
tributing to a self-sufficient empire. According to this view, the

---

[1] P. J. Thomas, *Mercantilism and the East India Trade; an Early Phase
of the Protection v. Free Trade Controversy* (London, 1926).

mother country, the sugar and tobacco colonies of the South, the bread and provision colonies of the North, the fisheries, and British Africa constituted a unified commercial entity consisting of diverse but cooperative members.

The ultimate advantage, of course, still accrued to the mother country, which since 1707 included Scotland. Ireland was largely barred from the direct plantation trade; the Channel Islands and Isle of Man were unimportant parts of the system. Barbados, Jamaica, and the Leeward Islands were prized for their sugar, molasses, rum, ginger, pepper, cotton, and dye-woods. The Carolinas, Virginia, and Maryland contributed tobacco, rice, indigo, naval stores, and furs. Pennsylvania, New York, and New England produced wheat, flour, bread, and livestock. The fisheries of Newfoundland and Nova Scotia were exploited exclusively for fish and neglected as places of settlement. Fisheries were especially valued as sources of sailors, and as helping to increase England's favorable balance of trade with Portugal by providing a commodity which could be traded for wines, oil, oranges and such, which Englishmen sought. This kind of trade relationship was especially important because France essentially barred English fish from French markets.

By the second decade of the eighteenth century, the collective value of all colonies was perceived by politician and merchant alike. A comprehensive view of the situation of colonies in England's commercial system, increasingly well-defined, helped to shape a complete body of regulations. Such regulations, raised almost to the level of principles, dominated English attitudes toward America right up to the Revolution.

Other attributes of English mercantile thought also developed alongside these colonial considerations. Advocates urged the ministries to encourage home manufactures, increase the productivity of the laboring force, and foster complete employment. Criminals, troublemakers, weak and lazy people would therefore be dispatched to America, on the assumption that there they would be magically regenerated as useful laborers and artisans. Encouraging manufacturing at home, of course, meant restricting it in the colonies. The Wool Act of 1699 was followed by others which meant to encourage native industries and discourage efforts overseas. The Hat Act of 1732, the Iron Act of 1750, and others virtually prohibited colonials from making hats and finished iron products and from refining sugar. The mercantilists' fear of American enterprise even induced them to prevent the export of artisans and their tools to the colonies.

One problem, never effectively resolved by either the government or the mercantilists, involved the need for an adequate money supply in the imperial dependencies. England was unwilling to provide any sort of coinage for its colonies, partially because of the mercantilist belief that money should come into rather than leave the realm. Minting a special set of coins for America would have been expensive, difficult, and a strain upon England's bullion supply. In fact, mercantile policy presumed that one useful function of colonies would be to channel Spanish and other foreign coins into the realm. Consistently, therefore, England even refused to permit a modest copper coinage for daily use in the provinces. At best the government simply regulated by proclamation and statute the value of foreign coins in terms of sterling. That colonial commerce suffered as a result is not surprising. There would soon be political repercussions as well.[2]

There was yet a negative side to English mercantile assumptions about the nature of colonies: they should not be costly to maintain. The government was willing, up to a point, to provide protection and defense. It necessarily had to pay the cost of all measures taken for preventing smuggling and breaches of the Navigation Acts. Indeed, such preventive measures also involved Ireland, the Channel Islands, the Isle of Man, and especially Scotland, where Virginia tobacco and French brandy were both illegally landed. Scottish challenges to the system, especially at Glasgow, became so infuriating

---

[2] Curtis P. Nettels, *The Money Supply of the American Colonies Before 1720* (Madison, Wis., 1934).

that in 1723 a separate board of customs commissioners was established at Edinburgh.[3]

"We have," wrote a pamphleteer in the early 1720's, "within ourselves and in our colonies in America an inexhaustible fund to supply ourselves, and perhaps Europe, with what we are now beholden to foreigners for, and that at the expence of our silver and gold; and yet either our negligence or private views make us sit still, and not improve what God and Nature have laid open to us." Opponents of the mercantile view argued that encouraging colonial trade would make the remote provinces dangerously rich and consequently independent. The same pamphleteer replied that such arguments "are only mists raised to hide the true reason, which is party opposition; for if our colonies could arrive to such greatness as to supply us with what is above recited, there would not a man in England want imploy in our manufactures, for its evident the gains and product of our colonies center here in England," and "their dependence will be their interest."[4]

This was the essence of mercantile thought through the Age of Walpole, especially with regard to colonies. As productive agricultural plantations, they furnished England with sugar, tobacco, naval stores, fish and other products. By direct shipment, as in the case of fish, and by re-exportation from England to other European countries, as in the case of enumerated commodities, they helped Britain's balance of trade, and, where desirable, made England independent of her neighbors. Nevertheless mercantile thought was not subscribed to by all, nor could the practice ever measure up to the program. British merchants and investors were often hurt by adverse governmental actions and colonial deviations. Many factors, at one

---

[3] Jacob M. Price, "The Rise of Glasgow in the Chesapeake Tobacco Trade, 1707-1775," *William and Mary Quarterly*, 3rd ser., XI (1954), 185-86.

[4] Quoted in Charles M. Andrews, *The Colonial Period of American History* (New Haven, 1934-38), IV, 364-65. I am especially indebted to Chapter 10 of this remarkable volume, subtitled *England's Commercial and Colonial Policy*.

time or another, undermined the supposedly self-sufficient mercantile system. Among the more important must be cited the failure of the sugar bill of 1731, the modified Molasses Act of 1733, New Englanders fishing off the banks of Newfoundland, new markets opening south of Cape Finisterre to sugar and rice, shipping to foreign countries colonial staples that until 1764 were not enumerated, and, of course, the colonial coastal trade. Mercantilists never realized—at least not until it was too late—that inadequate enforcement in America enabled the colonists not only to render the Navigation Acts ineffective but to violate or evade orders issued and laws passed in London.[5]

Beyond the mercantile system, unsystematic as it may have been, lay the complex world of European diplomacy, which also shaped the political economy of Britain's dependencies. Spain and France pursued policies similar to Britain's. The Treaty of Madrid of 1670, therefore, between England and Spain, provided that subjects of neither country should enter colonial ports of the other for purposes of trade. In consequence no colonist could legally trade with any port in the Spanish West Indies. If he did so, he risked confiscation of his ship and cargo. In 1686 England and France made a similar agreement. Neither treaty was faithfully observed, of course, despite efforts by home authorities. Jamaican captains brought large cargoes of English goods into Havana, Porto Bello, Cartagena, and other places along the Gulf of Mexico, where Spanish traders slipped out beyond the harbors at night in canoes to trade on a cash basis. Despite illicit activity, however, such international prohibitions did limit commercial opportunities for colonists, and had a serious effect upon the imperial money supply.

Until 1713 Anglo-French commercial relations were complex and inconsistent, alternating between free trade and close protection in 1678, 1685, 1686, 1689, 1696, and during the War of the Spanish Succession. Smuggling by French privateers

---

[5] Lawrence A. Harper, *The English Navigation Laws: A Seventeenth-Century Experiment in Social Engineering* (New York, 1939), Part 3.

and by residents of the Channel Islands went on continuously. For more than seventy years following the Treaty of Utrecht, Britain would maintain prohibitory duties on French goods. Since colonials could only obtain French fabrics, wines, and other products through England, such commodities (highly desired in eighteenth-century America), could best be procured through illegal trading with the French and Dutch West Indies and New France. In short, England's protective policy against France unquestionably heightened smuggling in America, England, Scotland, Ireland, and the Channel Islands.

The general level of duties covering England's import trade virtually quadrupled between 1690 and 1704. Such abrupt increases revealed and created in many specific sectors of the economy problems which had been unimportant when duties were lower. The government then sought to resolve such problems through a series of exemptions and modifications. These were of course achieved only after intensive lobbying by various interests involved, and inevitably led to pressures for additional measures, such as bounties and discriminatory duties. Between 1689 and 1704, therefore, the English tariff structure was transformed into a high-level fiscal system quite protective in orientation. It was then constantly and minutely modified in ways that heightened its protective nature.[6]

In 1713, as part of the peace settlement at Utrecht, proposals were offered to abolish the prohibitive duties which had arisen since 1689. But by 1713, as Professor Ralph Davis has shown, "new vested interests had grown up and protectionist ideas had developed, and between them may have exerted the decisive pressures that caused a House of Commons that was politically oriented towards making a long-term settlement with France to throw out these commercial clauses of the Treaty of Utrecht." After 1704 the raw materials of British industry were taxed heavily—between 15 and 25 per cent. Despite consider-

---

[6] Cf. George L. Cherry, "The Development of the English Free-Trade Movement in Parliament, 1689-1702," *Journal of Modern History*, XXV (1953), 103-119.

able pressures for adjustment and reduction, little was done. The government was strong enough, and the special interests divided enough, so that successive ministries withstood private pressures; concessions were made here and there at the discretion of government. In 1705 the drawback was removed from the reexport of foreign iron and ironware to the colonies —a victory for reexporters. Textile interests received a favor in 1714 with the abolition of duties on cochineal and some minor dye stuffs, and in 1718 through lowered duties on Turkish silk and mohair yarn. "In a number of cases of this kind," again in the words of Professor Davis, "we see issues being raised, comparisons being drawn, advantages for special interests being weighed and pursued, which would have been too trivial to attract attention in the seventeenth century, but which the ever-increasing rates of duty were giving substance to in the eighteenth."[7]

Sir Robert Walpole's customs reform of 1722 consolidated and rationalized thirty-two years of piecemeal concessions and protectionism. Industrial protection had formally become a policy of state. Thereafter, extensions of existing protections evolved as competitive interest groups lobbied effectively. They had much to gain by exemptions, for example, from tariffs on raw materials at the new high levels. But each exemption allotted to one interest only weakened resistance to pressures from other exemption-seeking interests.

The textile industries were especially powerful. Consequently, duties on flax and on Irish woolen yarn were abolished in 1732 and 1740 respectively. Duties on linen were reduced in 1752 and abolished four years later. Because of similar pressures between 1722 and 1742, export bounties were placed on English silks, sailcloth, and linen destined for certain foreign and colonial ports.

---

[7] Ralph Davis, "The Rise of Protection in England, 1689-1786," *Economic History Review*, 2nd ser., XIX (1966), 306-17. For the quotations see p. 313.

By the early 1720's the Board of Trade responded as sensitively as a weathervane to the needs of English merchants and the conditions of foreign trade as interpreted by those merchants. Particularly irksome were acts of provincial legislatures laying duties on English imports into the colonies. The Privy Council insistently instructed royal governors to veto such bills; and when they still slipped through, merchants clamored for disallowance.[8] By the 1740's the configuration of British and imperial political society had changed markedly. Various economic and social groups seeking to shape public life and public measures had become larger, louder, stronger, and better organized. In the last third of the seventeenth century and during the first third of the eighteenth, whenever the international situation became critical, narrow group interests were subordinated to the national interest. After 1739, especially, this ceased to be true, as we shall see.[9]

INTEREST POLITICS AND THE ORIGINS OF DISEQUILIBRIUM

In the four decades following the Glorious Revolution of 1688, certain dominant characteristics emerged in the history of British and colonial interest groups. Yet generalizations about these characteristics are predicated upon the configuration of groups themselves: which were emerging, which declining? Those traditionally strong, such as land, textiles, and iron remained so despite internal divisions.[10] Many overseas trading companies, however, declined[11] or, as in the case of the Darien

---

[8] Leonard W. Labaree, *Royal Government in America* (New York, 1958), pp. 60-63; Jack P. Greene, ed., *Settlements to Society, 1584-1763* (New York, 1966), p. 231.

[9] *Cf.* Sven-Erik Åström, *From Cloth to Iron: The Anglo-Baltic Trade in the Late Seventeenth Century* (Helsingfors, 1963), p. 186.

[10] J. H. Plumb, *Sir Robert Walpole: The Making of a Statesman* (London, 1956), pp. 20-21.

[11] Gerald B. Hertz, "The English Silk Industry in the Eighteenth Century," *English Historical Review*, XXIV (1909), 710-27; Charles H. Wilson, *England's Apprenticeship, 1603-1763* (New York, 1965), pp. 270-71.

Company, never really gathered momentum.[12] The Eastland
Company had its privileges curtailed in 1673, and was moribund by the later 1720's.[13] Its collaborator in the 1690's, the
Russian Tobacco Company, mostly Baltic merchants involved
in the naval stores trade, remained active throughout the eighteenth century, but declined with diminished political influence
following the Hanoverian succession.[14] The Royal African
Company lost its monopoly in 1698 and was steadily repressed
in politics for half a century until its revival in the 1750's. The
Levant Company underwent a similar decline in this period,
and the gradual demise of the South Sea Company after 1720
is well known.[15]

Others among the trading companies, especially those which
helped combat the French overseas, gained in strength, notably
the East India and Hudson's Bay Companies after the first
decade of the eighteenth century. During the long diplomatic
negotiations leading to the Treaty of Utrecht in 1713, the
Hudson's Bay Company reached its first apogee. Fortunately,
the Duke of Marlborough had been a governor of the Company, and was most sympathetic to its claims. Nonetheless in
1709 the General Court of the Company sent a member of its
London committee with a colleague to Holland to represent
its interests at the pending negotiations. Consequently, when

---

[12] Properly known as the Company of Scotland Trading to Africa and
the Indies, created in 1695 and intended as a rival to the East India Company. See George P. Insh, ed., *Papers Relating to the Ships and Voyages
of the Company of Scotland Trading to Africa and the Indies, 1696-1707*
(Edinburgh, 1924).

[13] R. W. K. Hinton, *The Eastland Trade and the Common Weal in the
Seventeenth Century* (Cambridge, Eng., 1959), p. 161.

[14] Jacob M. Price, *The Tobacco Adventure to Russia: Enterprise, Poli-
tics, and Diplomacy in the Quest for a Northern Market for English
Colonial Tobacco, 1676-1722, Transactions of the American Philosophical
Society*, new series, LI, part 1 (Philadelphia, 1961), pp. 38-41, 44.

[15] K. G. Davies, *The Royal African Company* (London, 1957); John
Carswell, *The South Sea Bubble* (Stanford, Calif., 1960).

the conference finally began, the Bay became one of Britain's irreducible terms.[16]

During the reign of Queen Anne, the Hamburg, Greenland, Turkey, and Russia Companies sought relief. Their complaints were ignored. The country was at war, and all attention was consequently focused upon the international struggle. Besides, the nation was financially insecure. In order to restore public credit, Robert Harley, Chancellor of the Exchequer and Tory leader of Her Majesty's government in 1711, devised a grand scheme for incorporating all the nation's creditors into a trading company, whose capital would be the national debt. Parliament incorporated the South Sea Company, therefore, as a means of restoring public credit and funding the national debt. An equally important motive was the English desire to expel the French from the trade of the Spanish West Indies. In that they succeeded. By the Treaty of Utrecht with Spain, the English supplanted the French in holding the Asiento grant, a contract to supply the Spanish West Indies with Negro slaves for a thirty-year period. According to the Asiento's terms, one-fourth interest was retained by the King of Spain, one-fourth went to Queen Anne, and the remaining one-half to an organized British company. The grant was procured by the South Sea Company, which was also to receive the Queen's share.[17]

The two decades following 1696, then, constituted a time of war, and therefore of much distress for most companies. It was also a period of intense friction between England and Scotland. The Scots had resented their exclusion by the Navigation Acts. To overcome their bitterness and gain a chunk of Britain's foreign trade, they formed their own trading company, The Scottish East India and African Company. It was

---

[16] E. E. Rich, "The Hudson's Bay Company and the Treaty of Utrecht," *The Cambridge Historical Journal*, XI (1954), 183-203. For the new and expanded role of imperial business interests in these years, see Gerald S. Graham, *The Politics of Naval Supremacy: Studies in British Maritime Ascendancy* (Cambridge, Eng., 1965), p. 18.

[17] Ancil N. Payne, *The Relation of the English Commercial Companies to the Government, 1660-1715* (Urbana, Ill., 1930), pp. 6-8.

bitterly opposed by commercial interests in London, who got Parliament to investigate and ultimately impeach the leaders and organizers of the Scottish Company for high crime and misdemeanor. In the face of such political opposition and influence, the Scots failed miserably.

During these same dour decades, craft gilds lost heavily in their effort to preserve their medieval hegemony over traditional manufacturing, especially to mercantile interests centered in London and even in Ireland.[18] Long underestimated by historians, it is now clear how active and significant the Irish lobby was in influencing British policy and legislation during the first third of the eighteenth century.[19] Simultaneously the West Indian, and with less vigor, the North American interests emerged during these years, along with a peculiar sort of interest, that of the dissenters. The latter "tended to become more distinct than other interests, for they were segregated by their political and social circumstances."[20]

William Penn had been the first Quaker lobbyist to grapple with the tangles of Anglo-American politics. From the late 1690's, despite having "greater Interest at Court now than ever hee had in King James Raigne," Penn was perplexed by the ever-shifting locus of decision-making for imperial dependencies. In 1700-1701 intensive efforts had to be made among Penn's friends in the House of Commons to forestall anticipated attacks upon private colonies. From Philadelphia Penn so instructed his London agent, Charlwood Lawton; and paradoxically the dissenting proprietor gained his greatest support among Tories in both houses. After an exhausting six-year struggle in concert with Sir Henry Ashurst, agent of Connecticut, and diverse parliamentary interests, Penn suc-

---

[18] Stella Kramer, *The English Craft Gilds: Studies in Their Progress and Decline* (New York, 1927), pp. 115, 139 ff.; Wilson, *England's Apprenticeship*, p. 269.

[19] Francis G. James, "The Irish Lobby in the Early Eighteenth Century," *English Historical Review*, LXXXI (1966), 543-57.

[20] Wilfrid Harrison, *Conflict and Compromise: History of British Political Thought, 1593-1900* (New York, 1965), p. 117.

ceeded in resisting efforts at imperial unification. His achievement was the more remarkable because by 1703-1704 his "influence at Court" was much reduced. He had lost touch with several important officials.[21]

The various dissenting interests often found politicking in the Age of Walpole frustrating, even when they cooperated with the establishment. Henry Newman, New Hampshire's agent from 1709 until 1737, helped Dean George Berkeley in 1725-1726 establish an Indian College in Bermuda. Although Berkeley "had a great deal of patience and courage with a powerful interest," their efforts failed. After Massachusetts appointed Jeremiah Dummer agent in 1716, Newman quickly discovered how capable and cunning his colleague could be. Boundary disputes and variant interpretations of the Bay Colony charter brought the two into constant conflict. In addition, Newman suffered from the agent's traditional woes of a miniscule salary, the high cost of effective lobbying, political feuding at home, and the uncertainty of his official authorization as colonial agent. Newman waited upon Walpole endlessly and ineffectually in quest of stores for Fort William and Mary. Along with other agents, Newman lamented the passage in 1729 of another naval stores bill making certain types of American timber inaccessible to colonials. At least the North American agents had prevented English ironmasters from adding in the committee stage a clause prohibiting the manufacture of bar iron in New England.[22]

A truly unified North American colonial interest never existed during the Age of Walpole. As early as 1707, both Englishmen and colonists agreed that "our strength is not only

---

[21] Alison G. Olson, "William Penn, Parliament, and Proprietary Government," *William and Mary Quarterly*, 3rd ser., XVIII (1961), 183, 185, 188, 190-95; Joseph E. Illick, *William Penn the Politician: His Relations With the English Government* (Ithaca, N. Y., 1965), pp. 154, 160, 165, 196-202, 207-10, 233-34.

[22] Leonard W. Cowie, *Henry Newman: An American in London, 1708-1743* (London, 1956), pp. 181, 203, 205-207, 209, 211, 221; Perry Miller, *The New England Mind from Colony to Province* (Cambridge, Mass., 1953), pp. 391-92.

divided and weakened, but by reason of their several interests
they are become and do in a manner esteem each as foreigners
to one unto the other, so that, whatever mischief does happen
in one part, the rest remain unconcerned."[23] Patronage and
trans-Atlantic influence shaped the careers and made the fortunes of such colonial officials and entrepreneurs as Samuel
Vetch, whose interests and investments cut across colonial
boundaries. They were unified by his political ties in London.
Privately he engaged in intercolonial trade and military supply;
publicly he was one of Queen Anne's leaders in the Glorious
Enterprise to capture Canada. Eventually he became the
Governor of Nova Scotia.[24]

The politics of mercantilism affected colonial interests in
various ways. One scholar has observed that "in the absence
of any crown policy for the empire more comprehensive than
the vague demands of mercantilism, Newcastle's [the secretary
of state after 1724] conduct of colonial affairs was dominated
by his obsession with patronage." Of course men appointed
to the colonial service were no better or worse than men
receiving domestic offices. They were all equally ambitious,
competent or incompetent. Yet "because of the unusual challenges that faced the colonial governors, the quite usual exercise of patronage in their appointment was responsible for a
serious weakening of the colonial administration."[25]

The politics of mercantilism also shaped and shattered individual colonial interests and economies. Fluctuating economic
conditions in such developing colonies as Virginia combined
with favoritism to English tobacco merchants had a profound
impact upon American life. The trans-Atlantic tobacco trade
was depressed and distressed by the 1720's, despite efforts by

---

[23] Quoted in Charles M. Andrews, *The Colonial Background of the
American Revolution* (New Haven, 1924), p. 15.

[24] G. M. Waller, *Samuel Vetch, Colonial Enterpriser* (Chapel Hill,
N. C., 1960).

[25] Stanley N. Katz, "Newcastle's New York Governors: Imperial
Patronage During the Era of 'Salutary Neglect,'" *New-York Historical
Society Quarterly*, LI (1967), 9-10.

English merchants and Virginia planters to revive it by legislative action. The persistence of these conditions led the Virginia planters to enact an effective tobacco inspection law in 1730, and induced the English tobacco merchants to secure an Act of Parliament in 1732 safeguarding debts owed them in America. Still more significant was Sir Robert Walpole's abortive project to convert the customs duties on tobacco into an excise. The Virginia planters supported such a scheme in vain, because the interested English merchants had the power and influence to defeat it. Virginia had been constricted into a a pattern of economic dependence, for the colonists lacked any measure of control over their own economic life. Virginia's failure to achieve a degree of economic maturity comparable to its political development would ultimately have profound significance.[26]

By contrast, the simple fact of Georgia's birth and colonization after 1730 owed much to the founders' success as parliamentary lobbyists. The current flair for organized philanthropy helped, as did the patriotic considerations involved. From the standpoint of practical politics, however, it is significant that many members of Parliament and other governmental officials were chartered, or later elected, as trustees of Georgia. Whereas private donations collected for the colony amounted to only £16,000, Parliament voted more than £136,000 in subsidies. The politics of Georgia's establishment and colonization were exceedingly complex and involved diverse interests. General James Oglethorpe had to unite his prominent trustees; obtain a grant of land; persuade the Privy Council; secure approval of Carolina's proprietors; and obtain Walpole's promise both to secure passage of an Enabling Act of Parliament, and to allow the project a share of the proceeds of the current state lottery. Even then the continued support of the elite community of entrepôt merchants of London became

---

[26] John M. Hemphill II, "Virginia and the English Commercial System, 1689-1733. Studies in the Development and Fluctuations of a Colonial Economy Under Imperial Control" (Ph.D. dissertation, Princeton University, 1964).

crucial to the colony's survival. Indeed in March, 1733, the Trustees selected several of the entrepôt merchants to join the Board. Once the colony was established, its maintenance obliged the Trustees to seek almost annual grants from Walpole and Parliament. These applications required the most concerted kinds of high-level lobbying by Oglethorpe and his associates, even including personal appearances before the House of Commons.[27]

GOVERNMENT AND THE EMERGENT INTERESTS

Among all the extra-parliamentary forces that emerged in British politics between 1690 and 1730, the greatest object of concern was called the moneyed interest: a complex network of groups whose appearance infuriated Jonathan Swift, Viscount Bolingbroke, and their many Tory contemporaries. The Revolution of 1688 had altered the character of government finance by leading to parliamentary control of taxation and specific funds designated for interest on loans. One result was the interdependence of government and its largest investors, a symbiotic relationship making each side highly sensitive to the other's needs. Short-term Exchequer bills and long-term annuities provided a variety of liquid securities for investment and for use as collateral security for loans.[28] Successive governments, therefore, cultivated relations with men in finance who formed a crucial link to the investing public. The underwriter's job, especially during recurrent wartime emergencies, was to apportion a block of stock from the new loan among his clients. These underwriters shortly constituted a powerful

---

[27] H. B. Fant, "Financing the Colonization of Georgia," *Georgia Historical Quarterly*, XX (1936), 28; Amos A. Ettinger, *James Edward Oglethorpe: Imperial Idealist* (Oxford, 1936), pp. 111-18, 120-25, 143, 149, 231, 237-39; Geraldine Meroney, "The London Entrepôt Merchants and the Georgia Colony," *William and Mary Quarterly*, 3rd ser., XXV (1968), 230-44.

[28] D. M. Joslin, "London Private Bankers, 1720-1785," *Economic History Review*, 2d ser., VII (1954), 169; P. G. M. Dickson, *The Financial Revolution in England* (London, 1967).

investing interest, interlocked by the personnel of their directors and boards.[29]

For Jonathan Swift the insidious moneyed interest seemed to comprehend not only banking and insurance people, but elements of the great companies as well. In 1721 he wrote to the poet Alexander Pope of his apprehensions on this account:

> I ever abominated that scheme of politicks (now about thirty years old) of setting up a mony'd Interest in opposition to the landed. For I conceived there could not be a truer maxim in our government than this, That the possessors of the soil are the best judges of what is for the advantage of the kingdom: If others had thought the same way, Funds of Credit and South-sea Projects would neither have been felt nor heard of.[30]

Bolingbroke's views, heated in the same crucible, were comparable and appeared with greater frequency. He too regarded the moneyed interest as a consequence of 1688, and remarked that "the landed men are the true owners of our political vessel; the moneyed men, as such, are but passengers in it."[31] His *Letters on the Study and Use of History*, written in the 1730's, reflected his distress at the changed balance of British political society.

> The notion of attaching men to the new government, by tempting them to embark their fortunes on the same bottom, was a reason of state to some: the notion of creating a new, that is, a moneyed interest, in opposition to the landed interest, or as a balance to it; and of acquiring a superior influence in the city of London, at least by the establishment of great Corporations, was a reason of party to others.[32]

---

[29] Wilson, *England's Apprenticeship*, pp. 320-21; Bernard Drew, *The London Assurance: A Second Chronicle* (London, 1949), p. 154; Dorothy Marshall, *Eighteenth Century England* (London, 1962), pp. 88-89.

[30] Swift to Bolingbroke, 14 Sept. 1714, to Pope, 10 Jan. 1721, Harold Williams, ed., *The Correspondence of Jonathan Swift* (Oxford, 1963-65), II, 129, 372-73. See also R. H. Tawney, *Religion and the Rise of Capitalism* (London, 1926), p. 207.

[31] Quoted in Sir Leslie Stephen, *History of English Thought in the Eighteenth Century* (3rd ed.; New York, 1962), II, 151.

[32] (2d ed.; London, 1792), pp. 38-39.

In *The Patriot King*, Bolingbroke's views were not tied exclusively to the landed classes, for he recognized the need for balance in government and economics. While he neither approved of nor trusted interest groups, he sensed their inevitability. Some members of society "propose to themselves a separate interest; and, that they may pursue it the more effectually, they associate with others."[33]

Bernard Mandeville, Bolingbroke's contemporary and a thorough mercantilist, shared many of these views, believing that legislators and politicians ought carefully to subordinate private interests to the common good, if necessary through systematic regulation of economic and social groups.[34] A third representative from this period, Daniel Defoe, uttered similar sentiments: "if inquiry after disorders at home should delay taking care of our safety abroad, if private clashings and disputes between parties and interests should take up the hours which are due to the emergency of foreign affairs, the people of England will be very ill-served." In Defoe's case, however, the shrewd propagandist was embellishing partisan proposals with the commonplace palliatives of his day.[35] No one would deny the primacy of Britain's interest over all others, but the consistency with which many flouted that maxim in practice was remarkable and would become even more so during the middle third of the eighteenth century.

Between 1690 and 1730 an uneasy standoff existed between government and the many interest groups, varying with the condition of parties, factions, public finance, and foreign relations. The presence of a party system and a reasonably strong executive generally forced interest groups to direct their ener-

---

[33] Sydney W. Jackman, *Man of Mercury: An Appreciation of the Mind of Henry St. John, Viscount Bolingbroke* (London, 1965), pp. 110, 136; *The Idea of a Patriot King*, in *The Works of the Late Right Honorable Henry St. John* . . . (London, 1754), III, 99.

[34] *A Letter to Dion* (1732), reprinted with an introduction by Jacob Viner (Los Angeles, 1953), pp. 1-15.

[35] "The Original Power of the Collective Body of the People of England Examined and Asserted" (London, 1701), in William Hazlitt, ed., *The Works of Daniel Defoe* (London, 1843), III, 11.

gies to the upper levels of government where only moderate and substantiated claims were likely to succeed. Hence the rather slow collective rise in influence of interest groups during the second and third decades of the eighteenth century, as Whig and Tory parties gave way to one amorphous and fragmentary Whig party. Under the last Stuarts interest groups placed their particular needs before the government. That body, however, had a will of its own and resisted being ruled by them, though it might listen sympathetically.[36] Occasionally it was vulnerable to special pleading. In consequence the woolen interests or the East India Company might briefly dictate policies of state, as in the late 1690's.[37] But on the whole such cases were not common, as ministers sought to keep the upper hand.

Under George I lapses might recur, as with the South Sea Bubble and its preliminaries prior to 1720. Even then, however, government pressure forced the powerful Bank of England to enter the negotiations.[38] In succeeding years adroit ministers played off the Bank and the South Sea Company, like ringmasters manipulating participants in the political arena.[39] In these years, it was the politicians who had the power to make or break the merchants, not vice versa. During his early ministry in the 1720's, Walpole adroitly granted or refused

---

[36] Hinton, *The Eastland Trade*, p. 164; Christopher Hill, *The Century of Revolution, 1603-1714* (Edinburgh, 1961), pp. 263, 267; William T. Morgan, "The Origins of the South Sea Company," *Political Science Quarterly*, XLIV (1929), 16-38; Morgan, "The South Sea Company and the Canadian Expedition in the Reign of Queen Anne," *Hispanic American Historical Review*, VIII (1928), 143-66; T. C. Barker, "Lancashire Coal, Cheshire Salt and the Rise of Liverpool," *Transactions of the Historic Society of Lancashire and Cheshire*, CIII (1952), 83-94.

[37] H. F. Kearney, "The Political Background to English Mercantilism, 1695-1700," *Economic History Review*, 2nd ser., XI (1959), 485, 495.

[38] Jacob Viner, "Clapham on the Bank of England," *Economica*, new series, XII (1945), 66.

[39] Lewis B. Namier, "Brice Fisher, M.P.: a Mid-Eighteenth-Century Merchant and His Connexions," *English Historical Review*, XLII (1927), 517, n. 2.

favors to tobacco contractors, craftsmen and artisans, North American agents and the like. By rejecting or tabling petitions which threatened his quest for stability, he kept the groups largely off balance.[40]

By the early 1730's, however, it was no longer clear who had the upper hand. Those groups excluded from policy considerations by more entrenched interests formed a kind of parliamentary or even extra-parliamentary opposition. Fear of war, high taxation, and the growing belief that England had been duped by France produced a coalition of interests against Walpole.[41] The result in 1733 was a stunning defeat for Sir Robert on the excise scheme. Merchants, especially those interested in wine and tobacco trades, mobilized public opinion. From all over England corporate towns sent deputations to London, newspapers and pamphlets discussed the issue, the City of London petitioned, and, ultimately, Walpole abandoned the scheme. The significance of 1733 was a preview of the role groups would consistently play following the peace of Aix-la-Chapelle in 1748.[42]

Even so, the vigorous activity of interest groups in British politics in 1733 was no isolated episode. The South Sea Company, with governmental support and without control or supervision, involved Walpole's ministry in its foreign quarrels, especially with the Spanish Crown. Between 1729 and 1739 its influence on Britain's foreign relations was in many instances determinative. After 1729, West Country fishing interests, especially the Newfoundland adventurers and merchants of Poole, agitated constantly against New England and Irish interference in the fisheries. Their complaints were not always heard sym-

---

[40] Wilson, *England's Apprenticeship*, p. 317.

[41] Price, *The Tobacco Adventure to Russia*, p. 100; Archibald S. Foord, *His Majesty's Opposition, 1714-1830* (Oxford, 1964), pp. 194-95; J. H. Plumb, *Sir Robert Walpole: The King's Minister* (London, 1960), II, Book One.

[42] *Ibid.*, pp. 231, 247, 252-53; Wilson, *England's Apprenticeship*, p. 317; E. R. Turner, "The Excise Scheme of 1733," *English Historical Review*, XLII (1927), 34-57.

pathetically, but in 1731 and 1732 were heeded, and they wielded considerable influence at the Board of Trade.[43]

The Irish lobby scored a great victory in 1731 when the Navigation Acts were revised to permit direct imports of unenumerated goods from the colonies to Ireland. The hatters triumphed in 1732, and the rapidly rising West Indian interest won passage of the Molasses Act in 1733 after a three-year campaign.[44] During the middle 1730's dissenters made repeated applications to Walpole for redress. The trustees of Georgia, seeking to bring pressure at this time for their new project, elicited the chief minister's exasperated dislike of "a body that hangs together and in parliament votes against the Government's measures."[45] As J. H. Plumb has suggested, Walpole "had no intuitive sense of dynamic political forces, for he held obstinately to a static view of society." In the 1730's he and others would deplore the excessive influence wielded by special interests. Power and wealth seemed "more dangerous in Numbers of Men joined together, in a Political Union."[46]

THE CHANGING MORPHOLOGY AND ROLE OF INTERESTS

By the 1730's interests clearly were playing a determinative role in British public life. "The technique of lobbying by interest groups had moved from the courtly fashion of the seventeenth century to the matter-of-fact pressure and influ-

---

[43] Ernest G. Hildner, Jr., "The Role of the South Sea Company in the Diplomacy Leading to the War of Jenkins' Ear, 1729-1739," *Hispanic American Historical Review*, XVIII (1938), 322-41; Ralph G. Lounsbury, *The British Fishery at Newfoundland, 1634-1763* (New Haven, 1934), pp. 277-90, 324.

[44] James, "The Irish Lobby," pp. 554-55; Penson, *The Colonial Agents of the British West Indies* (London, 1924), pp. 119-20, 122, 185.

[45] N. C. Hunt, *Two Early Political Associations: The Quakers and the Dissenting Deputies in the Age of Sir Robert Walpole* (Oxford, 1961); *The Journal of the Earl of Egmont*, Robert G. McPherson, ed., *Abstract of the Trustees Proceedings for Establishing the Colony of Georgia, 1732-1738* (Athens, Ga., 1962), p. 233.

[46] Plumb, *Walpole*, I, p. xiii; *A Collection of Papers Relating to the East India Trade* (London, 1730), pp. xi, xiii, xiv. See also Sir William Keith, *The History of the British Plantations in America* (London, 1738), p. 3.

ence of the eighteenth century. Henceforth," as Professor
J. M. Price has observed, "before the Treasury could propose
a new duty to parliament, it had to consider what interests
such a measure would affect, how strongly they were represented in parliament, and what resources of extra-parliamentary
pressure they had at their disposal."[47] One reason for the added
importance of lobbyists in politics lay in the fact that by the
1730's almost all major interests had well-organized bodies in
London to handle their affairs. A generation earlier many
interests had depended upon electing M.P.'s who might serve
them directly in Westminster. Therein lay the intensity of
East Indian participation in the election of 1701.[48] By the
same token the strength of England's woolen interest during
the later seventeenth century depended upon the size of its
parliamentary bloc. Organizational units of a permanent and
extraparliamentary nature were just beginning to take firm
institutional hold. An older lobby, such as the leather industry,
worked through a loose affiliation of merchants, tanners, and
graziers.[49] During William's reign the Russian Tobacco Company left its day-to-day political concerns in the hands of three
to five managers,[50] while the Hudson's Bay Company's London
structure of governor, deputy governor, and committee of
seven members remained constant.[51]

---

[47] Jacob M. Price, "The Tobacco Trade and the Treasury, 1685-1733:
British Mercantilism in Its Fiscal Aspects" (Ph.D. dissertation, Harvard
University, 1954), I, 19, 44.

[48] Robert Walcott, "The East India Interest in the General Election of
1700-1701," *English Historical Review*, LXXI (1956), 223-39.

[49] L. A. Clarkson, "English Economic Policy in the 16th and 17th Centuries: the Case of the Leather Industry," *Bulletin of the Institute of Historical Research*, XXXVIII (1965), 149-62.

[50] Price, *The Tobacco Adventure to Russia*, p. 29.

[51] John S. Galbraith, *The Hudson's Bay Company as an Imperial Factor,
1821-1869* (Berkeley and Los Angeles, 1957), p. 4. The naval stores interest comprised colonial commercial agents in London, tar merchants in the
colonies and England, rope makers, owners of American plantations and
others. See Kustaa Hautala, *European and American Tar in the English
Market During the Eighteenth and Early Nineteenth Centuries* (Helsinki,
1963), pp. 51-52.

In these cases the managerial staff of the interests served also as their political arms. By the early eighteenth century, however, numerous groups began to develop special personnel for lobbying. The Irish interest, for example, was represented in the Dublin Parliament and in Westminster by about a dozen M.P.'s, through churchmen such as Swift, Irish officials, and members of the Irish peerage. But in addition there also developed the London emissary of the Lord Lieutenant's chief secretary in Ireland, a position most comparable to the North American colonial agent. This operative was paid on a full-time basis to look after Irish affairs in London, and particularly to promote Irish commercial opportunities. In consequence the Irish lobby in Georgian England "was among the largest and most active pressure groups in London."[52]

The Irish linen industry created a board of trustees in 1710 whose function was to promote flax-growing and preparation, establish spinning schools, administer the linen acts, distribute bounties and prizes, and do everything possible to advance trade. For a long period, however, most members were substantial landowners, quite ignorant of trade, who infrequently appeared for meetings. As a result of pressure upon the government by the Convention of Royal Burghs and the Society of Improvers in the Knowledge of Agriculture, the Scottish Board of Trustees for Manufactures was established in 1727 to encourage industrial development there. Most of its political attention and subsidies were directed toward the linen industry.[53]

There were many other organizational and promotional bodies, such as Bristol's Society of Merchant Venturers, officials of the British Herring Fishery, and the City Corporation

[52] James, "The Irish Lobby," pp. 547, 550, 556.
[53] Conrad Gill, *The Rise of the Irish Linen Industry* (Oxford, 1925), pp. 65-66, 72, 80-81; R. H. Campbell, ed., *States of the Annual Progress of the Linen Manufacture, 1727-1754* (Edinburgh, 1964). See also Henry Hamilton, *An Economic History of Scotland in the Eighteenth Century,* (Oxford, 1963), pp. 133, 298-99.

for Liverpool. In 1734 a writer in the *Universal Spectator and Weekly Journal* referred to the frequent "Meetings of Clubs of particular Merchants, either fix'd or occasional, as of the Turkey and Italian Merchants, the Spanish, the Portuguese, the French, the Flanderçan, the German, the Danish, the Swedish, the Muscovite, the Dutch, the Irish, the West India, the Virginia, the Carolina, New York and New England Merchants."[54]

In the 1730's others were also created or strengthened that would play major roles in succeeding decades: the Protestant Dissenting Deputies, a committee of nine men working in London on behalf of Presbyterians, Independents, and Baptists; the committee of twenty-five London merchants selected for parliamentary opposition to Walpole's excise scheme, along with the London aldermen; and the Planters' Club, designed to promote West Indian interests along with the West India Committee. The latter met informally as necessity dictated and sought to influence legislation and regulate conditions for the sale and handling of sugar.[55]

By contrast with these vigorous and visible groups, the structure and influence of North American interests still seemed fairly frail. Two illustrations may suffice. In 1731 Daniel Dulany, Dr. Charles Carroll, Benjamin Tasker, Charles Carroll of Annapolis, and his brother Daniel formed a partnership, the Baltimore Company, in hopes of developing the trans-Atlantic iron trade. These Maryland merchants had well-established connections in London, the outports, and the West Indies. Their long struggle for influence and sales in England, however, reflects the weakness of an embryonic American com-

---

[54] Quoted in Penson, *The Colonial Agents of the West Indies*, p. 196.
[55] Hunt, *Two Early Political Associations;* Plumb, *Walpole*, II, 252-53; Lewis B. Namier and John Brooke, *The History of Parliament: The House of Commons, 1754-1790* (London, 1964), I, 137; L. M. Penson, "The London West India Interest in the Eighteenth Century," *English Historical Review*, XXXVI (1921), 373, 378-86; David H. Makinson, *Barbados: A Study of North American—West Indian Relations, 1739-1789* (The Hague, 1964), p. 75.

mercial interest. After two decades the amount of iron sold by the associates in England was about the same as for the early period 1734-1737.[56]

Lewis Morris, leader of the opposition faction in New York during the 1730's, had importuned friends and paid a professional agent in London to unseat Governor William Cosby in 1733-1734. These efforts failed, however, despite the fact that the agent was Ferdinand John Paris, a professional lobbyist and one of the most experienced Englishmen in colonial affairs. It therefore became necessary for Morris himself to undertake an arduous eighteen-month visit to accomplish his goal. In 1735-1736 Morris and his son presented their objections against Cosby as a complaint before the Privy Council. Because of the constitutional difficulties involved in gubernatorial politics, the Morrises were obliged to undercut Cosby's connections, as well as cultivate their own. Both were trying tasks. "It requires more time than you are aware of," Morris wrote, "before a man can . . . know which way to come at the great folks and have any tolerable acquaintance with them & tho I have had more advantage that way than perhaps any body that could have come from America, yet to tell you the truth I am as it were but walking in trammells yet and have not got my paces to perfection but come gayly on."[57]

Because Governor Cosby was not in London to defend his own interest, he relied upon agents and lengthy letters to state his case. James De Lancey, whose right to replace Morris as Chief Justice of New York was threatened by the fracas, took up cudgels for Cosby, as did De Lancey's kinsman, Sir John Heathcote, Baronet. By the summer of 1736, after eighteen months of bitter infighting, Morris found that he had achieved neither his personal objectives nor those of his New York fac-

---

[56] Keach Johnson, "The Baltimore Company Seeks English Markets: A Study of the Anglo-American Iron Trade, 1731-1755," *William and Mary Quarterly*, 3rd ser., XVI (1959), 37-60.

[57] Stanley N. Katz, *Newcastle's New York: Anglo-American Politics, 1732-1753* (Cambridge, Mass., 1968), pp. 51-55, 96, 100-2, 107-8.

tion. The Privy Council disapproved of Cosby's manner of removing Chief Justice Morris and ignored the Governor's request to suspend pro-Morris council members. Even so, the Privy Council would neither displace Cosby nor initiate constitutional reforms in New York. A weary, wiser Morris returned home with his mission largely a failure.[58]

During the War of the Austrian Succession (1739-1748), most influential London interests gained in strength. In 1744 the two West Indian groups as well as the colonial agents visited the homes of M.P.'s, soliciting their help against Henry Pelham's proposed sugar duties. They formed an alliance with Irish and Scottish lobbyists by offering as *quid pro quo* to support a tax on foreign linens. Their efforts—tremendously well unified and coordinated—succeeded. It is important to note, however, that their organizational front was still on an *ad hoc* basis. Not until the later 1750's would it become permanent.[59]

Meanwhile other groups were gaining steadily during the war years also. In fact the influence of a number of commercial interests on the conduct of the war was remarkable. Merchants and shipowners clamored for military protection, so that in 1742 a bill was introduced providing for the creation of a special trade protection squadron to cruise between England and Cape Finisterre. The proposal almost succeeded. During the forties London firms insured a large segment of the French maritime fleet against war risks. This, itself, is a stunning testimonial to the political influence of the English marine insurance companies. Despite protracted debate, Parliament refused to condemn the practice. The longer the war, the more significant the moneyed interests became as the government's paymaster. It was with good

---

[58] *Ibid.*, pp. 111, 131-32, 136.

[59] Penson, "The London West India Interest," pp. 379-81; Penson, *The Colonial Agents of the West Indies*, p. 120; Richard B. Sheridan, "The Molasses Act and the Market Strategy of the British Sugar Planters," *Journal of Economic History*, XVII (1957), 73-74.

reason, then, that in the 1750's shrill cries arose against the financial powers' excessive influence.[60]

As mid-century approached, contemporaries recognized the important roles played by interest groups in public life, and even understood their entrenched position in the very texture of political society.[61] One prominent politician, George Lyttelton, insisted publicly in 1739 that members of Parliament were elected not to represent special interests, but to speak for the nation as a whole. Others were compelled to reiterate his apprehensive view.[62] What no one quite yet realized was that a widespread series of changes would occur during the 1750's, changes so profound that by 1763 the structure and activity of interests would differ markedly from what they had been in 1748. During a dozen years the informal matrix of politics would be transformed.

---

[60] C. Ernest Fayle, "The Deflection of Strategy by Commerce in the Eighteenth Century," *Journal of the Royal United Service Institution,* LXVIII (1923), 282-84, 288-89; Jacob Viner, "Power Versus Plenty as Objectives of Foreign Policy in the 17th and 18th Centuries," *World Politics,* I (1948), 22, n. 53; H. W. Richmond, *The Navy in the War of 1739-1748* (Cambridge, Eng., 1920). For efforts by the West Country fisheries interest to oppose colonization in Newfoundland during the 1740's, see Lounsbury, *The British Fishery,* p. 247.

[61] See Shelburne's analysis, quoted in Lewis B. Namier, *England in the Age of the American Revolution* (2nd ed.; London, 1961), p. 191.

[62] Lyttelton, *Letter to a Member of Parliament From His Friend in the Country* (1739), quoted in J. Steven Watson, "Arthur Onslow and Party Politics," in H. R. Trevor-Roper, ed., *Essays in British History Presented to Sir Keith Feiling* (New York, 1964), p. 152.

CHAPTER 4

YEARS OF TRANSFORMATION, 1748-1763

British Politics and the Economy at Mid-Century

For most students of British history, especially economic history, the year 1750 has been a convenient dividing point between the pre-modern and modern eras. They usually find mercantilism moribund by then and the industrial revolution looming.[1] Obviously these changes were too vast, too sweeping to be pinpointed in time; to be sure, they lack a precise point of departure. Yet when those changes that can be chronicled are considered, evidence emerges which explains the transformation and turmoil of Great Britain's economy and political society during the 1750's. As one authority notes, "the years between 1748 and 1763 were a watershed in British imperial

---

[1] See Max Beer, *Early British Economics from the Thirteenth to the Middle of the Eighteenth Century* (London, 1938); W. H. B. Court, *A Concise Economic History of Britain, from 1750 to Recent Times* (Cambridge, Eng., 1954); William D. Grampp, "The Liberal Elements in English Mercantilism," *Quarterly Journal of Economics*, LXVI (1952), 465; D. C. Coleman, "Technology and Economic History, 1500-1750," *Economic History Review*, 2nd ser., XI (1959), 506-14; A. H. John, "Aspects of English Economic Growth in the First Half of the Eighteenth Century," *Economica*, new series, XXVIII (1961), 176-90; H. G. Hunt, "Landownership and Enclosure, 1750-1830," *Economic History Review*, 2nd ser., XI (1959), 497-505; W. O. Henderson, *Britain and Industrial Europe, 1750-1870* (Liverpool, 1954).

history and the starting point of the new imperialism."[2] Significantly the Treaty of Aix-la-Chapelle between Britain and France in 1748 was perhaps the last occasion before the era of William Gladstone when Britain voluntarily sacrificed territory for immediate trade advantages.

In British economic life, the end of the war in 1748 led to a remarkable resurgence. The export trade in iron, linen goods, and livestock products played an important part, reinforced by tremendous growth in the Irish and Scottish linen industries. The export of manufactures to the colonies, Ireland, and India accelerated with unexpected speed. In addition, new reexport trades grew to maturity. By 1750 England shipped Carolina rice and China tea in very large quantities; shortly West Indian coffee would be added. Certain temporary influences also heightened the economic expansion following the peace of Aix-la-Chapelle. These were the release of Spanish demands which had been pent up by nine years of war, reversal of England's long unfavorable trade terms with Portugal, and the export of surplus corn which reached its peak at this time.[3] Beginning in 1748 the London banking community experienced remarkably rapid growth. Between 1748 and 1756 half a dozen new banks were founded there; in 1758-1759 four more came into being. Such an accelerated expansion reflected in part the heightened economic activity of the 1750's. It also helped to sustain the "monied-interest" as a political entity in the City. All these factors in unison wrought economic and social changes of considerable magnitude between 1748 and 1756.[4]

---

[2] David Fieldhouse, "British Imperialism in the Late 18th Century: Defence or Opulence?" in A. F. Madden and K. Robinson, eds., *Essays in Imperial Government Presented to Margery Perham* (Oxford, 1963), p. 26; see also Lawrence Henry Gipson, *The British Empire Before the American Revolution* (New York, 1967), XIII, 182.

[3] Ralph Davis, "English Foreign Trade, 1700-1774," *Economic History Review*, 2nd ser., XV (1962), pp. 285, 288, 291-92, 295; T. S. Ashton, *An Economic History of England: the 18th Century* (London, 1955), pp. 3, 154, 183; H. E. S. Fisher, "Anglo-Portuguese Trade, 1700-1770," *Economic History Review*, 2nd ser., XVI (1963), 219-33.

[4] D. M. Joslin, "London Private Bankers, 1720-1785," *ibid.*, VII (1954) p. 173.

Even the resumption of war did not immediately break the trend. The years from 1757 to 1761 were characterized by economic vigor and prosperity, especially at home with the beginning of the canal age creating countless opportunities. A sudden increase in Scottish and Irish linen production after 1756 led to "irregular methods and disturbance of vested interests: [and] consequently to fresh regulation in order to preserve those interests." Vested interests in Ireland, such as the bleachers and drapers, secured between 1757 and 1764 three statutes imposing fresh restrictions on the work of weavers.[5]

Not surprisingly this burst of activity during the 1750's, especially investments in nonmilitary spheres, manifested itself in intensive private parliamentary lobbying. Private acts for turnpikes and enclosures increased at a fantastic rate after 1748, and their proponents were even more politically active than promoters of river navigation had been during the preceding half-century.[6]

	Turnpike Acts	Enclosure Acts
1702-1711 (10 years)	18	—
1713-1722 (10 years)	27	—
1729-1738 (10 years)	40	39
1739-1748 (10 years)	53	39
1749-1755 (7 years)	123	48
1756-1762 (7 years)	157	175

This trend would continue in the several decades after the Seven Years' War ended in 1763. Thus lobbying for private legislation came to occupy an enormous amount of time in the House, and almost every bill had the support of some special force. Hence in 1751 it was established that "any groups of particular interests promoting a bill must pay fees . . . to the

---

[5] Dorothy Marshall, *Eighteenth Century England* (London, 1962), pp. 241-42; Conrad Gill, *The Rise of the Irish Linen Industry* (Oxford, 1925), pp. 92-94.

[6] A. H. John, "War and the English Economy, 1700-1763," *Economic History Review*, 2nd ser., VII (1955), 340; T. S. Willan, *River Navigation in England, 1600-1750* (Oxford, 1936), pp. 28-51.

officers of the House, even though their bill, as in the Greenland fisheries case, might affect interests outside the group."[7]

Such a rule appeared to imply governmental hostility toward interests, but that was not necessarily the case. It was merely tacit recognition of the sheer number and competitive nature of new and refurbished groups that were politically active at mid-century. Henry Pelham, then effectively Prime Minister, was inclined to cooperate with them from 1749 until his death in 1754. Generally his government's policy encouraged and accommodated groups wherever possible.[8] Once the relative stability of the age of Walpole and Pelham ended in 1754, opportunities for interests increased even more. Pelham's brother, the Duke of Newcastle, was much too interested in patronage to bother with policy-making in public affairs. As instability increased later in the fifties, component groups within the government and opposition found advantage in forming connections with outside interests.[9] William Pitt, Newcastle's policy-oriented partner in the later 1750's, became one of the first chief ministers to use special interests adroitly as political ammunition and allies.[10]

The party system, loose as it was in the 1750's, involved *ad hoc* coalitions lacking permanency. Parties or factions existed primarily at election times, then dwindled in number and influence in between. Such weak and nonaggregative units reduced Parliament's effectiveness in making decisions. Significant political constellations tended to form around major interest groups, with the political process involving formal communication and the flow of influence between them.

---

[7] Lewis B. Namier and John Brooke, *The History of Parliament: The House of Commons, 1754-1790* (London, 1964), I, 183; J. Steven Watson, "Parliamentary Procedure as a Key to the Understanding of Eighteenth-Century Politics," *The Burke Newsletter,* III (1962), 121.

[8] Marshall, *Eighteenth Century England,* pp. 220, 231.

[9] *The Annual Register of the Year 1758* (3rd ed.; London, 1762), p. 10.

[10] Lewis B. Namier, *Crossroads of Power: Essays on Eighteenth-Century England* (London, 1962), p. 162; Lucy S. Sutherland, "The City of London in 18th-Century Politics," in Richard Pares and A. J. P. Taylor, eds., *Essays Presented to Sir Lewis Namier* (London, 1956), p. 64.

Tensions in these circumstances arose from the imperfect means of articulating and linking interests and from the diverse demands of interest groups channeled through the political system.

Hitherto latent interests, such as the welter of North American land companies,[11] the Scottish and Irish linen industries, or spokesmen for Lancaster and Liverpool,[12] appeared in London, but they lacked effective channels of expression. The information available to Whitehall and Westminster about the expectations and attitudes of these groups was neither complete nor accurate. Hence calculation was impossible. The flow of political interaction and discourse involved both underreaction and overreaction; and political latency alternated with rapid and almost unpredictable shifts in power and allegiance.[13]

THE CHANGING CONFIGURATION OF INTERESTS

Within this matrix of political and economic developments, the changing position and function of British interest groups assumed a special significance. The key word is indeed *change*. During the 1750's a striking number of interests emerged, underwent great stress, or ceased to be visibly prominent. Very few stood in influence and objectives at the end of the decade where they had in 1748. Mystical importance should not be ascribed to that particular year, however, for metal production had already gained because of incessant wars; the brew-

---

11 Julian P. Boyd, "The Susquehannah Company, 1753-1803," *Journal of Economic and Business History*, IV (1931), 38-69; Kenneth P. Bailey, *The Ohio Company of Virginia and the Westward Movement, 1748-1792* (Glendale, Calif., 1939).

12 T. C. Barker, "The Beginnings of the Canal Age in the British Isles," in L. S. Presnell, ed., *Studies in the Industrial Revolution* (London, 1960), pp. 16-17.

13 James F. Rees, "The Phases of British Commercial Policy in the 18th Century," *Economica*, V (1925), 150; C. P. Hill, *British Economic and Social History, 1700-1914* (London, 1957), pp. 94-96.

ing industry had been acquiring strength since the mid-1740's; while the shipping and indigo concerns began making great strides in 1747. Extensive lobbying in that year led to the Act of 1748 providing a bounty on all indigo manufactured in the British American plantations and sent directly "home."[14]

By mid-century, men in Britain who derived income from the complex slave-trading system had become a formidable pressure group in politics. Similarly their enemies, the Quakers on both sides of the Atlantic, devised very effective mechanisms for political action. The London Meeting for Sufferings had developed into an executive committee capable of dealing with important questions between yearly meetings. For some years Friends had been accustomed to the need for lobbying against discriminatory laws in England. They readily turned their attention to colonial legislation hostile to American Quakers. By 1750 the London Meeting had appointed a parliamentary agent as well as a standing subcommittee for parliamentary and colonial affairs.[15]

The East India shipping interest, consisting largely of shipowners and tradesmen in London, had made its influence strongly felt within East India Company affairs during the second quarter of the eighteenth century. In 1751 the shippers emerged dramatically as a distinct and vigorous group with organizational solidarity. In that year a group of thirty-one formally collaborated to pressure the Company into restricting the number of hired vessels. The resulting agreement remained in effect for more than a decade; thereafter the shipping interest sought and achieved still broader goals. Ordinary affairs of the group were attended to by a committee of two or three, while special negotiations were formally discussed and han-

---

[14] Charles Wilson, *England's Apprenticeship, 1603-1763* (New York, 1965), p. 309; Lawrence Henry Gipson, *The British Empire Before the American Revolution* (2nd ed.; New York, 1960), II, 125; Ralph Davis, *The Rise of the English Shipping Industry in the Seventeenth and Eighteenth Centuries* (London, 1962), p. 313.

[15] David Brion Davis, *The Problem of Slavery in Western Culture* (Ithaca, N. Y., 1966), pp. 154, 329.

dled by the full complement of thirty or more shippers and related merchants.[16]

The late 1740's signalled crucial turning points in the histories of most overseas trading companies. At opposite extremes were the South Sea Company, which died in 1748-1750,[17] and the Hudson's Bay Company which reached its political zenith about 1749. In March the House of Commons established a committee to investigate the Hudson's Bay Company's affairs, an inquiry that was pushed with some urgency because of petitions from all over the country urging that the Canadian fur trade be opened. In April the Company presented its defense, as well as a petition, on May 1, stating its case. Within a week the whole episode was closed. Having considered its committee's report, the evidence of witnesses, and the Company's appeal, the House of Commons saw no reason to interfere with the Company, whose hegemony over northern America was not seriously threatened for another decade. The Company was nevertheless on the defensive after 1752 when the hat industry pressured Parliament heavily for removal of the drawback allowed on reexported beaver pelts, or alternatively complete prohibition of their exportation. The hatters finally succeeded in 1764 despite protests from the Bay Company. Never again would its influence be quite as firm as in the spring of 1749.[18]

The Royal African Company, tottering for a generation, also came under attack in 1749 and collapsed. The newly cre-

---

[16] Lucy S. Sutherland, *A London Merchant, 1695-1774* (Oxford, 1933), pp. 88, 94-100, 109.

[17] Jean O. MacLachlan, *Trade and Peace With Old Spain, 1667-1750: A Study of the Influence of Commerce on Anglo-Spanish Diplomacy in the First Half of the Eighteenth Century* (Cambridge, Eng., 1940), chaps. 4-5.

[18] E. E. Rich, *The History of the Hudson's Bay Company, 1670-1870* (London, 1958-59), I, 583-84; Murray G. Lawson, *Fur: A Study in English Mercantilism, 1700-1775* (Toronto, 1943), pp. 21-26. For the unsuccessful attempt of Robert Charles, New York agent, along with the Bristol and London merchants, to break the monopoly of the Bay Company in 1749, see Nicholas Varga, "Robert Charles: New York Agent, 1748-1770," *William and Mary Quarterly*, 3rd ser., XVIII (1961), 227.

ated company which replaced it represented a different group of men who gradually emerged into a position of strength as virtually a new interest. After a thorough investigation, administrative management of commercial relations with West Africa was entrusted in 1750 to a Company of Merchants Trading to Africa. By statute this regulated company was placed under the control of a committee of nine representing London, Bristol, and Liverpool. Parliament would provide an annual subsidy for maintenance of the West African forts, and the Board of Trade would exercise general powers of report and investigation over the Company's trading policy. At first the Board vigorously exerted its supervisory functions, as did Parliament each year when the annual grant had to be considered. By the later 1750's, however, government supervision had become spasmodic. Through its financial leverage Parliament had every opportunity to impress its wishes or policies on the Committee, but it did so infrequently. During the fifties the African interest gained very considerable political strength, and would maintain its power through the later seventies. Its connections in Parliament and at the Board of Trade were notable and continuously useful. Meanwhile its economic growth, with the exception of 1755-1758, was steady from 1750 through the outbreak of the American Revolution.[19]

In 1753 the Levant Company underwent a transformation similar to that of the African Company three years earlier. A flood of petitions came from manufacturing towns to Parliament to open up the Levant trade. A rejuvenated Company would hopefully restore the cloth trade to those areas. To this end, Parliament willingly complied. An Act of 1753 broadened the Company's membership, delegated new responsibility to its General Court, and permitted appeals to the Board of Trade. Although the Company never achieved the political influence of the African or West Indian merchants during this period, it

---

[19] Eveline C. Martin, *The British West African Settlements, 1750-1821* (London, 1927), pp. 16-18, 27. I am also indebted to Mr. Dennis Klinge, Ph.D. candidate in history at Cornell University, for his excellent research essay, "The African Company in Parliament, 1750-1783."

regained economic viability for another two decades and received parliamentary favors when the need arose. Its revival during the mid-1750's temporarily reversed another downward trend of the previous decade.[20]

Early in the 1750's, then, a curious pattern unfolded. Parliament took an engrossing interest in affairs of the large trading companies. But having legislated some back to life and established a framework of regulatory controls, it then proceeded, willfully or not, to act permissively, letting the companies flourish with almost no supervision. In the case of Britain's iron manufacturers, 1750 heralded a crucial parliamentary victory: the famous Iron Act. Actually the Act had been delayed for some years because so many self-interested groups made contradictory demands: furnace owners hoping to raise duties on colonial pig iron; forge owners interested in obtaining pig iron duty-free from America; manufacturers of secondary iron wares seeking bar iron from America without tariff; shipping interests and woolen merchants with similar requests who believed the results would stimulate their trade. As one contemporary observer noted, "so many jarring interests prevented the legislature from doing anything at this time." The compromise act that emerged from this tangle in 1750 most favored the London iron manufacturers. Bar and pig iron would be admitted duty free in London but not the other ports, while slitting and plating mills in America were restricted.[21]

After just a few years, shippers and merchants of other British cities began to demand equal status with London in the admission of colonial bar iron without duty. The outbreak of war in 1756 provided a golden opportunity for these rising urban interests because the two great iron-producing countries, Sweden and Russia, aligned with France. In 1756 Bristol's

---

[20] Alfred C. Wood, *A History of the Levant Company* (Oxford, 1935), chap. 9.

[21] Arthur C. Bining, *British Regulation of the Colonial Iron Industry* (Philadelphia, 1933), pp. 57, 62, 65, 68-72, 115; Keach Johnson, "The Baltimore Company Seeks English Subsidies for the Colonial Iron Industry," *Maryland Historical Magazine*, XLVI (1951), 27-43.

Society of Merchant Venturers petitioned Parliament, along with iron manufacturers in Bristol, Birmingham, Liverpool, and several other cities. Meetings were held. Pamphleteering became the order of the day. Tanners, leather manufacturers, and owners of forges and woodlands rallied to the support of London's opposition. Finally, a bill allowing importation of colonial bar iron duty-free into all ports of Great Britain passed both houses and received crown approval in 1757. It was indicative of the imbroglio of intensely active interest groups during the mid-1750's.[22]

Tension between London and the outports was not restricted to the importation of iron. Liverpool's trade by 1750 surpassed Bristol's and made it second only to London's. By the century's end, Bristol's trade underwent a marked decline; at mid-century, however, the downturn seemed only a relative loss and the port retained considerable political influence. Along with Lancaster, Birmingham, and Manchester, the proliferation of urban areas active in politics by the 1750's was unprecedented in British history. Yet their increased numbers by no means reduced London's commerce, for each port stimulated the others' growth.[23] London's political weight was also augmented. Although it had led extra-parliamenary opinion in the 1730's and 1740's, the City had done so in conjunction with opposition politicians. By 1750, however, an important change occurred as London began to adopt political attitudes independent of parliamentary proddings. By 1751, after several years of supporting William Pitt, London acquired tremendous

---

[22] Bining, *The Colonial Iron Industry*, pp. 74-76.

[23] G. D. Ramsey, *English Overseas Trade During the Centuries of Emergence: Studies in Some Modern Origins of the English-Speaking World* (London, 1957), pp. 161-62; Bryan Little, *The City and County of Bristol: A Study in Atlantic Civilization* (London, 1954), chap. 7; Walter E. Minchinton, "Bristol—Metropolis of the West in the Eighteenth Century," *Transactions of the Royal Historical Society* 5th ser., IV (1954), 69-89; W. H. Chaloner, "Manchester in the Latter Half of the Eighteenth Century," *Bulletin of the John Rylands Library*, XLII (1959), 40-60; *An Essay on the Increase and Decline of Trade, in London and the Out-Ports* . . . (London, 1749).

self-confidence as a political force. What began as a financial interest became a determinative factor in national affairs.[24]

Problems in deciding the civil status of aliens early in the 1750's illustrated just how volatile and important the City had become. In 1751 Pelham supported a naturalization bill which Bristol and other commercial centers also favored. It was bitterly opposed in London, however, and consequently dropped in 1752. A year later, the Sephardic Jews, led by their wealthiest members working with government officials friendly with Jewish bankers and merchants, lobbied against the tax and strain Jews bore by being classed as aliens. Opposition came from London liverymen and merchants who felt the bill threatened their Iberian trade. The ministry passed it nonetheless, with support from elements in the commercial communities, especially outside London. Tory high churchmen and menaced City merchants raised such a hue and cry, however, that the administration repealed the Act before the elections of 1754.[25]

In part London's new strength was due to the presence of so many West Indian merchants and absentee planters, a group whose power reached its zenith between 1730 and the 1760's. Theirs was the largest business of any traders in London. For three years after 1748 their disputes with the North American colonies raged unresolved in London's offices and coffeehouses. Beginning in the fifties, the sugar-refining industry demanded free trade in raw sugars and abolition of the monopoly tax placed on English consumers and refiners. Toward the decade's end, the West Indian interest consolidated its organizational front behind the Society of West India Merchants, perhaps inspired by the Society of London Merchants trading

---

[24] Donald Read, *The English Provinces c. 1760-1960* (London, 1964), p. 6; Lucy S. Sutherland, "The City of London and the Devonshire-Pitt Administration, 1756-57," *Proceedings of the British Academy*, XLVI (1960), 147-93.

[25] Thomas W. Perry, *Public Opinion, Propaganda, and Politics in Eighteenth-Century England: A Study of the Jew Bill of 1753* (Cambridge, Mass., 1962).

to Virginia and Maryland, organized about the same time.[26] Cohesion became increasingly vital to the West Indian interest after 1755 because at that time its ten-year-old alliance with the Scottish and Irish linen interests was finally disrupted.[27]

Both of those groups felt expansive during the 1750's. Efforts to create a linen supply in the Scottish highlands were afoot, as the Scottish Board of Manufactures received from Parliament a special grant of £3,000 toward this end, good for a period of nine years. Soon after 1750 the Irish Board of Trustees for the linen industry came alive after a dormant decade and a half. One factor was the removal in 1753 of bounties for the export of linen from England. Since the British Parliament had withdrawn support, the Trustees felt special efforts were required in Ireland. Their ability to present a stronger front was reduced, however, by contentious groups within Ireland, particularly the bleachers and drapers who sought restrictions upon the weavers.[28]

Political as well as commercial changes affected the Irish interest at this time. The emergence in 1753 of a confrontation between the Irish administration and Parliament in Dublin stirred Irish public opinion as no event had since 1725. An attempt by the British government to intimidate opposition leaders by a display of power was shortlived. Tranquillity was restored in Ireland only after new offices and pensions had been distributed. Although the Duke of Newcastle recognized that the struggle began as a power dispute between rival groups in the Irish Parliament, he lacked the determination to turn the

----

[26] L. M. Penson, *The Colonial Agents of the British West Indies* (London, 1924), p. 124; Penson, "The London West India Interest in the 18th Century," *English Historical Review*, XXXVI (1921), 381-82.

[27] Richard Pares, *War and Trade in the West Indies, 1739-1763* (Oxford, 1936), pp. 509-11.

[28] Gill, *Irish Linen Industry*, pp. 93-95; *Hints Relating to Some Laws That May Be for the Interest of Ireland to Have Enacted. In a Letter to a Member of Parliament* (Dublin, 1749). Restrictions against the export of Ireland's cattle, sheep, butter, and cheese to England and the colonies were also lifted at mid-century. See Basil Williams, *The Whig Supremacy, 1714-1760* (Oxford, 1939), pp. 279-80.

situation to England's advantage. By accepting rather than dictating the settlement, he permitted the Irish interest to thrive. It would continue to do so for several decades.[29]

This catalytic period also affected the concerns of artisans and gilds, though only in the case of the gilds was the result immediately obvious. By mid-century the gilds' political strength was totally exhausted, for they could not confine local trade and industry to free gildsmen. Restrictions on the number of apprentices and the employment of foreigners were abolished. After 1750 quarterly meetings in many cases were discontinued for lack of attendance,[30] and in 1753, to take one example, Parliament destroyed the monopoly of the Company of Framework Knitters. In large measure it responded to petitions from the Midlands' stocking industry and completed the Framework Knitters' decline into a journeymen's organization.[31] During the Age of Walpole—the 1720's, 1730's, and 1740's—government had exerted a comparatively judicious but rigorous legislative control over labor combinations. After 1749 that control became positively repressive to the working class, and stimulated serious unrest in succeeding decades.[32]

The landed interest, of course, remained strong during this transitional period, though its presumptive priority over all

<hr />

[29] J. L. McCracken, "The Conflict Between the Irish Administration and Parliament, 1753-56," *Irish Historical Studies*, III (1942), 159-79; *The Free-Citizens' Address to Sir Samuel Cooke, Bart. for His Unshaken Attachment to the True Interest of Ireland This Session of Parliament....* (London, 1754); *Reasons for an Agent in England to Take Care of The Interest of Ireland in the Parliament of England. In a Letter to a Member of Parliament* (Dublin, 1756).

[30] Stella Kramer, *The English Craft Gilds and the Government* (New York, 1905), pp. 142, 177; George Unwin, *The Gilds and Companies of London* (4th ed.; London, 1963), pp. 346, 351. In 1751 a committee of the House of Commons reported strongly against compulsory apprenticeship. See Ashton, *Economic History of England*, p. 224.

[31] Jonathan D. Chambers, "The Worshipful Company of Framework Knitters (1657-1778)," *Economica*, IX (1929), 322-24.

[32] J. H. Plumb, *England in the Eighteenth Century* (London, 1950), p. 15; Gipson, *British Empire Before the American Revolution*, XI, 197-98; Eric Hobsbawn, "The Machine-breakers," *Past and Present*, I (1952), 66.

other major interests lacked its former certainty.[33] While some writers continued to assert the interdependence of all interest groups in public life—stressing that favors to, say, the leather trade, were good for agriculture—their pleas lacked the conviction of an earlier generation. Many publicists no longer bothered with such casuistry.[34]

The advent of the Seven Years' War profoundly affected two major interests: the Iberian trade and the East India Company. Even before 1756, Spain and Portugal had begun to foster their own industries, so that their demand for English manufactures slackened. The Cadiz and Lisbon trade, regarded by many British merchants as a single network, became unstable during the war, and never really recovered.[35] A new era began for the East India Company between 1748 and 1758 when the first great contested election occurred for control of the Court of Directors. These internal struggles marked the appearance of new strains and stresses destined to disrupt the

---

[33] Donald G. Barnes, *A History of the English Corn Laws from 1660-1846* (London, 1930), pp. 24-26; Philip W. Buck, *The Politics of Mercantilism* (New York, 1942), pp. 108-9.

[34] Malachy Postlethwayt, *The Universal Dictionary of Trade and Commerce* . . . (London, 1757), I, iv, II, 15; *The State of the Corn Trade Considered: In Answer to all the Objections Against the Bounty Granted to Encourage the Exportation of Corn, and Its Influence on the Landed and Navigation Interest . . . Explained* (London, 1753); [Joseph Massie], *Considerations on the Leather Trade of Great Britain . . .* (London, 1757). In John Rutherfurd's personal preface to Lord Halifax, written in 1760, he contended that "if the connection betwixt the landed and commercial interests in Britain with her colonies were made more mutually advantageous by Parliament . . . to give all possible encouragement to the colonists to grow, and to our merchants to import, such materials for manufacturers as at present cost us vast sums . . . that it would not only tend greatly to the enrichment of Britain, but in time render us independent of the world in point of trade." *The Importance of the Colonies to Great Britain . . .* (London, 1761), reprinted in William K. Boyd, ed., *Some Eighteenth Century Tracts Concerning North Carolina* (Raleigh, N. C., 1927), p. 109.

[35] *Mercators Letters on Portgual and Its Commerce* (London, 1754); Ralph Davis, "English Foreign Trade, 1700-1774," *Economic History Review*, 2nd ser., XV (1962), 288, n. 5; Allan Christelow, "Great Britain and the Trades from Cadiz and Lisbon to Spanish America and Brazil, 1759-1783," *Hispanic American Historical Review*, XXVII (1947), 2-29.

Company. In its relation to national politics, the crises of the Seven Years' War brought the first serious breach in the strength of its connections. After 1760 the Company's fortunes took a sharp turn for the worse. East Indian affairs, like North American, reentered party politics, and entanglement of the two in an age of "interest politics" proved disastrous.[36]

One other interest might be mentioned in connection with changes growing out of war: the Bank of England. During the first half of the eighteenth century, its publicly circulated notes dominated the world of finance, partially owing to conservative management and partially to strong government ties which gave great security to all its issues. Until the 1750's the Bank's directors (predominantly London merchants and merchant-bankers) concerned themselves primarily with profitable governmental business. Not until the wars and financial crises that followed 1756 could the Bank break the monopoly on discounts and mortgage loans controlled by other London investors.[37] Throughout this period the Bank's formal relations with the state were soothed and smoothed through annual gifts to Exchequer officers. By 1763 the Bank had taken over state finances almost completely, by custom rather than law, and the interaction of Bank and state was unobtrusive because it was so institutionalized.[38]

Colonial and imperial bureaucrats in America also found their English connections redirected or unsettled after the late 1740's, so that the traditional imperial politics of interest was much altered at mid-century. Admiral George Clinton, Governor of New York after 1743, found that simple intercession by English authorities could not solve the colony's difficulties as in 1736. Although Clinton's English connections were excellent on paper, in fact Newcastle could not help him effec-

---

[36] Lucy S. Sutherland, *The East India Company in Eighteenth-Century Politics* (Oxford, 1952), pp. 49-51.

[37] Joslin, "London Private Bankers," pp. 170-75; Viner, "Bank of England," *Economica*, new series, XII (1945), 61-66.

[38] Sir John Clapham, *The Bank of England: A History* (New York, 1945), I, 53-103.

tively, especially after 1748 when the Duke transferred from the Southern Department to the Northern, thereby foregoing responsibility for colonial affairs. By contrast, Clinton's opposition, the De Lancey interest in New York, had adequate influence in England through family relationships and commercial ties. Consequently merchants engaged in American trade, especially in furs, supported De Lancey's policy of peace and opposed Clinton's attempts to finance a war against the French. Indigenous American interests might operate effectively in London against shakily superficial transplants. Neither could compete very effectively, however, with the carefully organized English-based lobbies.[39]

The Reverend Samuel Davies, a leader among colonial Presbyterians, journeyed to England and Scotland late in 1753 in order to seek financial support for the young College of New Jersey in Prince Town. Unfortunately colonial Presbyterianism was then ideologically split into the New York and Philadelphia synods; and in England the dissenters were also divided. This confused state of affairs partially explains the relatively cool treatment Davies received from English Presbyterians. To make matters worse, William Smith, provost of the Philadelphia Academy, was also in London seeking support for a new college in New York City. Characteristic of the relatively frail, fragmented, private, colonial interests active at the Empire's center, the two clerics openly clashed and worked at cross-purposes.[40]

THE CHANGING LANGUAGE AND PERCEPTIONS OF POLITICS

During the sixth decade of the eighteenth century, then, virtually every interest group or type of interest underwent alterations of vast significance: internal changes, changes in relation

---

[39] Stanley N. Katz, *Newcastle's New York: Anglo-American Politics. 1732-1753* (Cambridge, Mass., 1968), pp. 200-203, 207-208.

[40] George W. Pilcher, ed., *The Reverend Samuel Davies Abroad: The Diary of a Journey to England and Scotland, 1753-55* (Urbana, Ill., 1967), pp. xi, 57-60.

to each other, changes in relation to politics and to the state. The attendant transformation in British and imperial politics had far-reaching implications, and belies Professor Gipson's portrayal of a calm, untroubled system at mid-century.[41] As testimony to the rapidity and intellectual impact of these changes, by 1755 the language of politics and of political economy had begun to change. In that year Sir James Steuart began writing his *Political Oeconomy*, becoming the first British writer of note to use that term. Steuart discerned two major eras in recent history. In the first, economic development had perceptibly affected political institutions. In the second, and more contemporary, processes of economic development had permanently begun to alter the balance of political power. "Every interest in a state," he argued, "must influence the government of it in proportion to its consequence and weight."[42]

In 1755 another literary occurrence testified to the importance of interest groups in public life. Dr. Johnson's famous *Dictionary* recognized that without indulging in semantical archaeology the word "interest," apart from its purely financial usage, had become a common though diversely used element in the King's English. Etymological dictionaries had appeared in almost every decade since the late seventeenth century, and in them the meaning of "interest" had remained singular, limited, and constant: "concernment, part or share in anything, advan-

---

[41] Gipson has presented this interpretation in volumes 1-3 of his *British Empire Before the American Revolution* (2nd ed.; New York, 1958-1960), and in his Harmsworth inaugural lecture, published as *The British Empire in the Eighteenth Century: Its Strength and Its Weakness* (Oxford, 1952), especially p. 23. Richard Pares acknowledges the activity of diverse interests at mid-century but minimizes their significance for national politics. See *King George III and the Politicians* (Oxford, 1953), pp. 3-4.

[42] S. R. Sen, *The Economics of Sir James Steuart* (Cambridge, Mass., 1957), p. v; A. S. Skinner, "Sir James Steuart: Economics and Politics," *Scottish Journal of Political Economy*, IX (1962), 20-21, 29; William Letwin, *The Origins of Scientific Economics* (New York, 1964), pp. 233-34. For the tremendous proliferation of economic literature in Britain during this period, much of it for, by, and about interest groups, see Henry Higgs, comp., *Bibliography of Economics, 1751-1775* (New York, 1935).

tage or power." Nathan Bailey's *Universal Etymological English Dictionary*, which underwent countless editions during the first half of the century, never deviated from these uses.[43]

With Johnson's *Dictionary* came more subtle nuances, supported by illustrations taken from Clarendon, Swift, and other writers of note. And in the case of Swift's usage there could be no question of his, and Johnson's, sensitivity to the presence of interests in political society.[44] In 1759 William Rider's *New Universal English Dictionary* contained an expanded, more sophisticated explanation of "interest": "concern, advantage, or good influence over others. Share, or part in any understanding in which our advantage is closely connected. A regard to private or personal advantage or profit." Subsequent eighteenth-century dictionaries followed Johnson and Rider in presenting the meanings of this ambiguous yet constantly used expression.[45]

During the late 1750's, the role played by interests became a national obsession, leading John Mitchell to remark that his countrymen felt "interest rules all the world."[46] In 1757 and 1758 John Brown's *Estimate of the Manners and Principles of the Times* became a best-seller because it so captured the spirit of the day. He feared the destruction of national unity by "selfish views and separate Interests." In his critique of public mores, "a *Chain* of *Self-Interest* is indeed no better than a *Rope of Sand:* There is no *Cement* nor *Cohesion* between the Parts: There is rather a mutual *Antipathy* and Repulsion. . . ." The

---

[43] Edward Phillips, *The New World of Words: or, Universal English Dictionary* . . . (6th ed.; London, 1706); Edward Cocker, *Cocker's English Dictionary* . . . (3rd ed.; London, 1724); Elisha Coles, *An English Dictionary* . . . (London, 1732); Bailey's *Dictionary* was first published in 1721.

[44] Johnson, *A Dictionary of the English Language* . . . (London, 1755), I.

[45] See the dictionaries by D. Fenning (4th ed.; 1771), William Kenrick (1773), John Ash (1775), Thomas Dyche and William Pardon (1777), James Barclay (1782), and George W. Lemon (1783).

[46] *The Contest In America Between Great Britain and France, With Its Consequences and Importance* . . . (London, 1757), p. 66. For the parallel reaction in Ireland, see *The Temple of Interest: A Poem Inscribed to His Grace the Lord Primate* (Dublin, 1754).

basic problem, in Brown's reckoning, was that "no public Measure, however salutary, can be carried into Act" if it clashed with private interests.[47]

Writing in 1757, like Mitchell and Brown, the publicist Malachy Postlethwayt produced a massive work, *Britain's Commercial Interest Explained and Improved; in a Series of Dissertations on Several Important Branches of Her Trade and Police.* . . . He devoted his first chapter to a discussion of the landed interest; his second and sixth to the Scottish, Irish, and North American interests; his seventh and eighth to the commercial interests of Britain; and his tenth to "the landed and trading interests connectively considered." Altogether these two volumes, with more than 1,100 pages, provided the most elaborate analysis in British history of her domestic, imperial, and colonial interest groups. Perhaps even more striking is the fact that a work of such monstrous bulk was read, for within eighteen months a second edition appeared.[48]

In 1757 Postlethwayt also produced an essay on *Great Britain's True System* in which he discussed the threat posed by increasing taxes and public debts to "the monied, the trading, and the landed interests." In his enormous *Universal Dictionary of Trade and Commerce*, whose second edition appeared in 1757, the author enumerated the major interest groups, discussed their relative strengths, alignments, and thrust in public affairs. The public debt, in his view, was largely responsible for the proliferation of interest groups "that we have lately suffered by, and, if not remedied, can have no end. It is the interest of the stock holders to involve the nation in War, because they get by it: it is the interest of landed men and merchants to submit to many evils, rather than engage in war, since they must bear the chief burden of it: and, however contemptible one may think the weight of the former, in com-

---

[47] *Estimate of the Manners* (London, 1757; Boston, 1758), pp. 55, 62-63, 67; "John Brown," *Dictionary of National Biography*.

[48] E. A. J. Johnson, *Predecessors of Adam Smith: The Growth of British Economic Thought* (New York, 1937), chap. 10.

parison of that of the latter, it was their superior influence that involved the nation in the late frivolous war with Spain."[49]

In general, then, Britain's more astute observers during the Seven Years' War warned against permitting diverse competitive interests to place their individual needs ahead of national policy considerations.[50] Horace Walpole, that sharp-eyed and sharp-tongued critic, did not "care a farthing for the interests of the merchants. . . . I am a bad Englishman, because I think the advantages of commerce are dearly bought for some, by the lives of many more. This wise age counts its merchants, and reckons its armies ciphers—but why do I talk of this age?— every age has some ostentatious system to excuse the havoc it commits."[51]

In the American colonies these same years also brought an awakening to the changing role of interests in public life. John Brown's *Estimate of the Manners and Principles of the Times* was purchased as enthusiastically in Boston as in London. In 1756 one prominent provincial observed that "Interest often connects people who are entire strangers, and sometimes separates those who have the strongest natural ties."[52] Another lamented that the thirteen colonies behaved like so many "different Interests";[53] and Benjamin Franklin wondered whether American representatives in Parliament might not serve to counteract "the private interest of a petty corporation, or of any particular set of artificers or traders in England, who heretofore seem, in some instances, to have been more regarded

---

[49] *Universal Dictionary*, II, 284-89.

[50] Jacob Viner, "Power Versus Plenty, as Objectives of Foreign Policy in the 17th and 18th Centuries," *World Politics*, I (1948), 18-19.

[51] Walpole to Sir Horace Mann, 26 May 1762, in W. S. Lewis *et al.*, eds., *Horace Walpole's Correspondence with Sir Horace Mann* (New Haven, 1960), VI, 39.

[52] James Alexander to Peter Van Brugh Livingston, 11 Feb. 1756, in Martha J. Lamb, *History of the City of New York* (New York, 1877-1880), I, 658n.

[53] Archibald Kennedy, *Serious Advice to the Inhabitants of the Northern Colonies* (New York, 1755), p. 15.

than all the Colonies, or than was consistent with the general interest. . . ."[54]

A generation earlier Jeremiah Dummer, New England's agent, had argued that Britain's economy depended upon the well-being of colonial economic interests. A perfect correspondence, in his view, existed between America's welfare and Britain's.[55] By 1754, when Franklin analyzed this same problem, a growing uneasiness was apparent. What did it matter, he asked, "whether a merchant, a smith, or a hatter grow rich in *Old* or *New* England?"

Franklin sensed increasingly that the North American colonies were at the mercy of Britain's various interest groups. Facets of colonial trade, he wrote from London in 1759, offended "the Trading and Manufacturing Interest; and the Landed Interest begin to be jealous of us as a Corn Country that may interfere with them in the Markets to which they export that commodity." A reading of David Hume's essay, "Of the Jealousy of Trade" (1758), prompted Franklin to write the author in 1760 that free trade would have "a good Effect in promoting a certain Interest too little thought of by selfish Man, and scarce ever mention'd; so that we hardly have a Name for it; I mean the *Interest of Humanity*."[56] American observers noted with alarm that an age of interests had begun in British politics.[57]

They would also perceive rather quickly the shift of America's commercial role in the Empire, just as Britain's economy

---

[54] Franklin to William Shirley, 22 Dec. 1754, in Leonard W. Labaree *et al.*, eds., *The Papers of Benjamin Franklin* (New Haven, 1962), V, 449-50.

[55] Dummer, *A Defense of the New-England Charters* (London, 1721), pp. 38-40.

[56] Franklin to Shirley, 22 Dec. 1754, *Papers of Franklin*, V, 449-51; Franklin to Isaac Norris, 19 March 1759, *ibid.*, VIII, 295-96; Franklin to Hume, 27 Sept. 1760, *ibid.*, IX, 229.

[57] See Charles F. Mullett, ed., "A Planter's Protest Against Any additional Tobacco Duty, 1759," *Journal of Southern History*, VIII (1942), 386-92.

was beginning to undergo a profound transformation. Expansion in the sheer volume of British productivity had slowed between 1725 and 1745, but gathered increasing momentum in succeeding decades. After the 1740's, increased agricultural development, a rise in population, and technological innovation facilitated rapid commercial growth. Even before these simultaneous occurrences, the "Americanization" of English foreign trade had begun. This overreaching structural transformation involved a series of investment booms on both sides of the Atlantic in shipbuilding, ports, the timber industry, and manufactures.[58] Even so, these changes would not necessarily work to the colonies' advantage. Before 1750 they exported more than they imported, and received cash in return. After 1755, however, imports from Great Britain began to exceed colonial exports. By 1760 the balance in Great Britain's favor amounted to nearly two million pounds. It would reach almost three million by 1770. After 1755 the goods exported to America from Britain were more than sufficient to pay for the staples furnished by the colonies.[59]

Thus fundamental changes in the structure of the economy and in the configuration of interest groups during the 1750's, as well as attitudes toward them, formed a prelude to the political chaos of the 1760's. The process of interest fragmentation, realignment, and aggressive behavior, completed well before the close of the Seven Years' War, set the stage for the subsequent political deterioration. The cohesion and administrative equilibrium needed to deal with the crises of the sixties and seventies might have been mustered had not the transformation of the fifties occurred. In this sense, the immediate origins of the American Revolution may perhaps lie not in 1763, or 1760,

[58] Phyllis Deane and W. A. Cole, *British Economic Growth 1688-1959: Trends and Structures* (Cambridge, Eng., 1962), chap. 2; Brinley Thomas, "The Dimensions of British Economic Growth," *Journal of the Royal Statistical Society*, CXXVII (1964), 116.

[59] Charles M. Andrews, *The Colonial Background of the American Revolution* (New Haven, 1924), pp. 101, 108.

CHAPTER 5

AN AGE OF INTERESTS, 1763-1783

The two decades separating 1763 and 1783 may properly be called an age of interests, for they so dominated politics that men observed that mercantilism had changed from the control of trade in the interest of national policy, to the control of national policy in the interest of trade. As Professor Guttridge has noted, the increasing importance of Parliament seemed to encourage efforts by powerful groups seeking to influence regulation by political pressure.[1] Spokesmen for the Old Whigs believed it their function while in office to reconcile the "jarring and dissonant" interests, to serve as arbiters among them, and they attempted to do so in 1765-1766. In 1774, when Lord Shelburne sent his analysis of the deepening American crisis to Lord Chatham, he first discussed the positions of various interests, and only as an afterthought turned to "parties and particular men." When the war had dragged its bloody

---

[1] G. H. Guttridge, *English Whiggism and the American Revolution* (Berkeley, 1942), p. 58; Dora Mae Clark, *British Opinion and the American Revolution* (New Haven, 1930), pp. 99, 253; see also Lewis B. Namier, *The Structure of Politics at the Accession of George III* (2d ed.; London, 1960), p. 18.

course longer than most groups were willing to indulge, a combination of interests "influenced Parliament to reorganize the government and end the war."[2]

During these years nearly every sphere of public life—whether domestic, imperial and international politics, economic theory, or social cohesiveness—was sharply tested and shaken. "Our Government has become an absolute Chimera," the philosopher David Hume remarked in 1769; "So much liberty is incompatible with human Society. . . ." In his troubled view, control of the ship of state had slipped out of the grasp of "the King, Nobility, and Gentry of this Realm."[3] The government was susceptible as never before to pressures from interests, whose success depended largely on their influence and financial strength, the administration's particular weakness at a given moment, and what other groups were then active and aggressive.

In a period of such dangerous instability, interest groups had the power to force or help force ministerial resignations, as colonial land companies discovered in 1772 when they helped topple Lord Hillsborough as Secretary of State for the American Department. More important, the search for stability led administrations to seek every available prop to bolster the system; hence the particular support given to traditional interests regarded as bulwarks of government, such as the East India Company.[4] Nevertheless the quest for allies and equilibrium caused administrations to be dragged into the imbroglio of

---

[2] Edmund Burke, *A Short Account of a Late Short Administration* (1766) in *The Works of . . . Edmund Burke* (London, 1899), I, 266; Shelburne to Chatham, 4 April 1774, in William T. Taylor and John H. Pringle, eds., *Correspondence of William Pitt, Earl of Chatham* (London, 1838-40), IV, 341; Clark, *British Opinion*, p. 150. See also Horace Walpole, *Journal of the Reign of George III, from the Year 1771 to 1783*, ed. John Doran (London, 1859), I, 326.

[3] Hume to William Strahan, 25 Oct. 1769, in J. Y. T. Greig, ed., *The Letters of David Hume* (Oxford, 1932), II, 210.

[4] Lawrence H. Gipson, *The British Empire Before the American Revolution* (New York, 1965), XI, 449, 474; Bernard Donoughhue, *British Politics and the American Revolution: The Path to War, 1773-75* (London, 1964), pp. 23-24; Benjamin W. Labaree, *The Boston Tea Party* (New York, 1964), pp. 13, 258, 260.

interests, and Parliament no less so. A factionalized and undisciplined party system opened the legislative process as never before to covert interest group domination of legislative committees and agencies, as well as propagandistic maneuvers. Private bills passed through nineteen stages in the House of Commons, so that on many bills the House as a whole had little notion of what was happening. Committees were the effective and instrumental organ in the legislative process and were invariably staffed by the very M.P.'s with personal stakes in the particular legislation being considered.[5]

A party system commonly stands between interest groups and authoritative policy-making bodies, screening them from the particularistic and disintegrative impact of special interests. When parties are strong they tend to inhibit the capacity of private groups to make specific demands. When the groups dominate, as they did after 1763, they inhibit the ability of parties to combine specific interests into programs with wider appeal. Since no interest group is large enough to have a majority, and the factionalized party system cannot aggregate diverse interests into a stable majority and a coherent opposition, the result is, and was then, a splintered legislature dominated by relatively narrow interests and uncompromising tendencies. This legislature could serve as an arena for propaganda, or for protection of special interests, but not for effective and timely formulation and support of large policy decisions.

Moreover, with the party system in Parliament unable effectively to articulate and regulate interests, that process gravitated in part to the bureaucracy, thereby diminishing its capacity for responsible administration. Under these circumstances the bureaucracy tended to be multifunctional: it responded to and coordinated interest groups, making policy for them and helping to administer it. When the bureaucracy

---

[5] Ninetta S. Jucker, ed., *The Jenkinson Papers, 1760-1766* (London, 1949), pp. 106-7, 145-46, 231-32, 274; J. Steven Watson, "Parliamentary Procedure as a Key to the Understanding of Eighteenth-Century Politics," *The Burke Newsletter*, III (1962), 123-24.

became weakened, as with the American Department after 1772, a system resulted in which the agencies of political choice failed to function, and in which basic policy decisions could not be made. Government became a task of protection and maintenance in which the effective bodies were special interests and parts of the bureaucracy. The latter was "colonized" by interest groups and penetrated by incompatible demands.[6]

Rapid economic growth of the sort that occurred in Britain after mid-century is likely of itself to be a source of political instability. When that phenomenon occurs for other reasons as well, as it did during the 1760's, the combination can be volatile in most extraordinary ways. Accelerated economic growth and the quest for political harmony involve deep changes in the way policy is made, where it is made, and in the distribution of power and prestige. All these interrelated characteristics were in motion during the 1760's.[7]

Private Power and Public Policy: An Inventory of Interests

Even the landed interest was shaken by turmoil. Ministries continued to placate it by keeping the land tax low, but in contests with other forces in politics its dominance could no longer be taken for granted. Constituent elements widened or shifted their concerns, thereby altering the total group's political goals. Just as it became more difficult to absorb rising groups outside the landed interest, it was awkward or impossible to present political views broad enough to satisfy all those seeking or achieving power. Conflicts with the West Indian interest became serious toward the close of the Seven Years'

---

[6] For a broad conceptual discussion of these problems, see Gabriel A. Almond, "A Comparative Study of Interest Groups and the Political Process," *American Political Science Review*, LII (1958), esp. 275-76, 280. For the bureaucracy, see Franklin B. Wickwire, *British Subministers and Colonial America, 1763-1783* (Princeton, 1966), *passim*.

[7] See Mancur Olson, Jr., "Rapid Growth as a Destabilizing Force," *Journal of Economic History*, XXIII (1963), 529-52.

War. By 1766 opposition against concessions to the North American colonies was strongest among the landed interest, but with mixed results.[8]

In 1768 came the judgment of one observer: "The landed interest is beat out, and merchants, nabobs, and those who have gathered riches from the East and West Indies stand the best chance of governing this country." Two years later Sir John Molesworth, supporting a motion for disabling revenue officers from voting in parliamentary elections, remarked: "Those tools of any Administration have prevailed over the spoils of the East, have prevailed over all family connexions, all the landed interest."[9] Older publicists and writers on commercial affairs, such as John Campbell, pleaded that the landed and trading interests were not antithetical, despite efforts by some to make them seem so. He urged that the best way to obviate such talk was to make the ties between the two more clearly visible. Despite these alarms, however, the landed interest remained a tremendous force. When in 1772 a bill was presented in Parliament eliminating any bounty on exported corn, the House rose in a fury to defeat it. The act which passed a year later made nominal changes and took away no real advantage the landed classes had enjoyed in practice throughout the century.[10]

The iron industry gained political cohesion during these years. Disputes pitting merchants and iron manufacturers of London, Birmingham, Wolverhampton, Walsall, and other towns against Sheffield iron- and steel-makers, were lessened after 1763 by the general clamor for bounties on importations of American iron. An act of 1764 made iron an enumerated commodity, virtually forcing colonial producers to send their

[8] J. Steven Watson, *The Reign of George III, 1760-1815* (Oxford, 1960), pp. 153-54; G. E. Mingay, *English Landed Society in the Eighteenth Century* (London, 1963), pp. 10, 264; Richard Pares, *War and Trade in the West Indies, 1739-1763* (Oxford, 1936), p. 509.

[9] Quoted in Namier, *Structure of Politics*, pp. 64, 155, 167.

[10] Campbell, *A Political Survey of Britain . . .* (London, 1774), II, 723; Donald G. Barnes, *A History of the English Corn Laws from 1660-1846* (London, 1930), pp. 41-44; C. R. Fay, *The Corn Laws and Social England* (Cambridge, Eng., 1932), p. 34.

iron to Great Britain. It was hardly surprising, then, that West Midland iron manufacturers supported American agents seeking repeal of the Stamp Act in 1765-1766, for disastrous losses in American business loomed. Interestingly, though, their views would be reversed in less than a decade.[11]

British merchants trading to Lisbon and Cadiz encountered serious difficulties during these years, and in consequence made powerful demands upon the government for assistance. After 1763 threats to British commerce by Iberian light industries became a matter of state policy. Consequently British ambassadors to Madrid and Versailles were instructed to protest the commercial partiality being shown to France. Numerous complaints from English merchants led the Board of Trade to conduct an elaborate survey of British trade in southern Europe. British traders with Portuguese America protested so loudly about their exclusion from certain routes and ports that Chatham's government in 1767 even considered the possibility of war with Spain and Portugal. Similar demands and threats persisted into the 1770's.[12]

The troubled affairs, civil and commercial, of the East India Company also elicited great governmental concern. In 1762-1763 the Company arranged with the ministry just what demands should be made in peace negotiations with the French. The Company first produced a statement of terms acceptable to it and then appointed a secret committee to persuade the government to adopt them. The treaty in its final form satisfied the Company, and relations between it and Whitehall improved in the next few years. Nonetheless, Company affairs really regained national prominence because factional contests within it became entangled with parliamentary battles raging over

---

11 Arthur C. Bining, *British Regulation of the Colonial Iron Industry* (Philadelphia, 1933), pp. 79-82; R. A. Pelham, "The West Midland Iron Industry and the American Market in the Eighteenth Century," *University of Birmingham Historical Journal*, II (1950), 141-62.

12 Allan Christelow, "Great Britain and the Trades from Cadiz and Lisbon to Spanish America and Brazil, 1759-1783," *Hispanic American Historical Review*, XXVII (1947), 13-16, 24, 28-29.

terms of the peace. These internal disputes gradually worsened, inducing Chatham in 1766-1767 to initiate a parliamentary
inquiry and obtain three acts affecting the Company's powers.
Its stock immediately boomed, but the relationship between
parties within the Company and factional alignments in Parliament also intensified. The former sought support from both
the government and its opposition, which in turn pursued the
same course with their own political ends in view. After 1767
it was impossible for the state to extricate itself from the Company's snarled affairs, the more so. in 1772 when East India
speculators helped bring on the great financial crisis of that
year.[13] The culmination of their interplay came in Boston late
in 1773, when a certain party brought the brewing crisis to a
boil. Instead of oil upon troubled waters, there was tea.

Other overseas trading companies held steady during these
years, staving off threats and seeking protection. While the
most perilous era for the Hudson's Bay Company actually
began in 1784 with the emergence of the North West Company,
the earlier Peace of Paris was followed by confrontations with
rival British traders. In 1764 Hillsborough's plan for management of North American Indians and the fur trade was
designed to safeguard the Bay Company's chartered rights.
Dissatisfaction among the Indians, however, along with pressure from hatters and furriers, led to a loosening of controls in
1765.[14] The Levant Company's quasi-revival after 1753 was
rather precarious, and the outbreak of war shattered its prosperity in 1775. During the later 1760's and early 1770's, the
Company applied to the government for financial aid, and the
House of Commons authorized the crown to make annual

[13] Lucy S. Sutherland, *The East India Company in Eighteenth-Century
Politics* (Oxford, 1952), pp. 55-56, 94-99, 138, 147, 150, 157, 177, 191, 223,
269; Richard B. Sheridan, "The British Credit Crisis of 1772 and the American Colonies," *Journal of Economic History*, XX (1960), 161-86.

[14] Gordon C. Davidson, *The North West Company* (Berkeley, 1918),
p. 5; E. E. Rich, *The History of the Hudson's Bay Company, 1670-1870*
(London, 1958-59), II, 12-14; Wayne E. Stevens, *The Northwest Fur
Trade, 1763-1800* (Urbana, Ill., 1926), p. 8.

grants. Ministerial ties to the Company were strengthened by their sharing of consulates in the East, with the Company often paying the salaries of some officials.[15]

The African Company was far stronger and more successful during these years. In 1763 it won valuable concessions through the peace treaty. Between 1768 and 1775 both Lords Hillsborough and Dartmouth as chairmen of the Board of Trade complied with requests from the Committee of African Merchants to intervene on their behalf in the Anglo-Dutch coastal quarrel. The Committee expressed its gratitude to the Board in 1774 for "the very great care you have been pleased to take of the interests of the British merchants during the whole of the negotiations." In 1772 Sir William Meredith led a parliamentary attack on the Committee, charging it with corruption and laxness in administering West African forts. Though he proved his case effectively, his bill to regulate the Committee failed to pass because of Edmund Burke's shrewd defense of the Committee. He made Meredith's criticisms appear as an assault upon individual liberty which would give a few rich traders monopolistic control. Burke and others staved off still another attack in 1777 by contending that the Committee did an admirable job of supporting the forts with limited funds. Lord North ultimately intervened on the Committee's behalf, and deferred proposals for closer control of African affairs.[16]

Throughout the fifteen-year period following the accession of George III, the African interest worked quietly, efficiently, and flexibly to achieve its goals, assisted greatly by firm connections in both Westminster and Whitehall. Traces of the former antagonism between London and the outports remained hidden beneath the surface, concealed by the financial support London investors and brokers provided for Liverpool's slavers. Much of the interest's success was due to the strength of its

---

15 Alfred C. Wood, *A History of the Levant Company* (Oxford, 1935), pp. 158-66.
16 Eveline C. Martin, *The British West African Settlements, 1750-1821: A Study in Local Administration* (London, 1927), pp. 19-26.

organizational front. The annually elected committee of nine managed to achieve continuity of personnel and became a semi-permanent body, illicitly increased in number to sixteen by ignoring provisions of the Act of 1750. Members of the Committee were intimately familiar with the best procedural methods in communicating with secretaries of state, commissioners of trade, and Exchequer employees. They drafted memorials for these offices, carried on negotiations, and assured even greater stability by informally creating a permanent secretariat.[17]

The West Indian interest perhaps achieved its maximum strength during the 1760's. A sizeable and powerful bloc of its M.P.'s sat in the Commons, greatly feared and resented by the North American agents. Its extra-parliamentary structure also crystallized during these years, when the Planters' Club expanded its activities and membership to include not only planters but merchants trading in West Indian produce. Differences between these two elements were minimized after 1764, the year the American Sugar Act passed. Thereafter the interest began its long, slow decline, becoming less aggressive and more concerned with prevention of measures prejudicial to the Caribbean.[18]

The Irish linen weavers also reached a crest in activities in 1763-1764, when they fought efforts by merchants and drapers in Belfast, London, Bristol, and Liverpool seeking greater regulation of Irish linen, particularly its quality. A pamphlet

---

[17] Richard B. Sheridan, "The Commercial and Financial Organization of the British Slave Trade, 1750-1807," *Economic History Review*, 2nd ser., XI (1958), 249-63; Martin, *West African Settlements*, pp. 29-30.

[18] Israel Mauduit to ?, 3 March 1764, Massachusetts Archives, LVI, 412-13, State House, Boston; Eric Williams, *Capitalism and Slavery* (Chapel Hill, N. C., 1944), p. 97; David H. Makinson, *Barbados: A Study of North American-West Indian Relations, 1739-1789* (The Hague, 1964), p. 75; Lillian M. Penson, "The London West India Interest in the Eighteenth Century," *English Historical Review*, XXXVI (1921), 385-86; Penson, *The Colonial Agents of the British West Indies* (London, 1924), pp. 124-25, 195-96; Lowell J. Ragatz, *The Fall of the Planter Class in the British Caribbean, 1763-1833* (New York, 1928), pp. 144-69, 183.

war in 1762-1763 preceded passage of the Act in 1764, which proved to be a pyrrhic victory for English merchants. They soon protested rules governing the length and breadth of medium and coarse linen. Between 1764 and 1780 the Irish Board of Trustees for the Linen Industry met irregularly, its finances became confused, and it gave lavish subsidies without proper inquiry. Nonetheless its supporters in London remained active, particularly Viscount Clare early in the 1770's. In 1779 the interest of many Trustees and M.P.'s concerned with Irish trade was quickened by the negotiations for greater freedom in Anglo-Irish commerce. In 1782 the entire system of administration by the Board of Trustees was reformed. The Irish had consistently sought free trade for their linen. Although the legislation of 1782 did not help immediately, it did climax a three-year campaign, allayed fears, and consolidated national feelings.[19]

The two decades after 1763 were active ones generally for the Irish interest. It maintained agents in London as links between Whitehall and the Viceroy in Dublin. These agents, whose function was to keep the crown informed on Irish affairs, were of two kinds: specialists sent on an *ad hoc* basis, usually for several weeks, and a permanent agent who remained continuously in England except for occasional briefings in Dublin. The career of Thomas Allan, Lord Townshend's London agent from 1769 until 1772, and occasionally Lord Harcourt's between 1773 and 1777, is instructive. Allan's role was a sensitive and important one, for as he wrote in 1770, "some person is wanted to get publick business through the Offices, as no sort of trouble is taken about it." Extensive preparations by Allan and the British undersecretaries preceded any cabinet meeting on Irish affairs. On many such

---

[19] Conrad Gill, *The Rise of the Irish Linen Industry* (Oxford, 1925), pp. 113, 116, 198, 201, 211, 219-20; Claud Nugent, *Memoir of Robert, Earl Nugent* (Chicago, 1898), pp. 266-67. See also Francis G. James, "Irish Colonial Trade in the Eighteenth Century," *William and Mary Quarterly*, 3rd ser., XX (1963), 580.

occasions Allan was even present to answer questions. His access to the King, Lord North, the Secretary of State, and other ministers was relatively easy, as was his entry into the parliamentary galleries.[20]

In 1770-1771 Allan had the difficult task of persuading the cabinet to consent to Townshend's administrative policies, particularly patronage control. Conscientious and efficient, intimately acquainted with British and Irish affairs, Allan persuaded North's new government to agree to the Viceroy's major changes. Although the English really did not understand the political situation in Ireland, Allan persuaded the cabinet to consider it at great length. In 1771 the agent even won a victory over the powerful West Indian agents by having the duty on rum altered. Once again close cooperation with North paid dividends. The agent may also have been partially responsible some years later for an act allowing free importation of woolen yarn from Ireland into England.[21]

The political consciousness of London and the outports, augmented in weight and authority by the 1750's, reached full flower in succeeding decades. The problem of colonial paper currency, for example, provoked successful remonstrances in 1763-1764 from London, Glasgow, and Liverpool's merchants, who hired their own attorneys to represent their cases in Whitehall and Westminster. Manchester also began to emerge in these years, and the City of London, by leading the opposition to the cider excise in 1763, not only firmed up a decade's political growth, but established an alliance with the western

---

[20] Edith M. Johnston, *Great Britain and Ireland, 1760-1800: A Study in Political Administration* (Edinburgh, 1963), pp. 81-84, 87-88. Unlike the North American agents in 1770, Allan was not only admitted to the gallery but conferred there with subalterns sent by Lord North to get information and advice on Irish policy while debates proceeded on the floor. The agent and the administration found mutual value in such cooperation (Edith M. Johnston, "The Career and Correspondence of Thomas Allan, c. 1725-1798," *Irish Historical Studies*, X [1957], 313).

[21] *Ibid.*, pp. 298-324; *The History of Lord North's Administration, to the Dissolution of the Thirteenth Parliament of Great Britain* (Dublin, 1782), pp. 318-19, 363.

counties as well.[22] The London "crowd" in these years provided a useful adjunct to the urban area's new strength and by the late sixties had to be considered a potent force in public affairs. It had not yet developed its own organization and leaders, but was manipulated by such figures as John Wilkes to "operate on behalf of external interests"—the wealthy tradesmen, merchants, and manufacturers of the City who were Wilkes' most influential supporters.[23]

Elsewhere in England, especially after 1765, widespread hunger riots and price-fixing riots became common. Most of these, signalling the rise of labor as an independent political force, were aimed at reducing the prices of wheat, barley, or their derivatives. In many cases, the rioters pressured private vendors, but often they also tried to force local magistrates to sanction their demands officially. In 1766, when an outburst of near-nationwide rioting peaked, a royal proclamation enforced Elizabethan statutes regulating dealers, as a concession to the hungry, restive populace. In 1772, however, these restrictive measures were abandoned, although common-law provisions against monopolists might still be invoked.[24]

One of the most remarkable political achievements of labor agitators in this period involved use of public discontent and disorder in reducing the level of protectionist corn laws. In 1773, following severe disturbances, the export bounty and the import price threshold were both lowered somewhat. Even before that date the landed interests had not reaped the full benefit of high prices during years of scarcity because Parlia-

---

[22] Lawrence H. Gipson, "Virginia Planter Debts Before the American Revolution," *Virginia Magazine of History and Biography*, LXIX (1961), 269-70; W. H. Chaloner, "Manchester in the Latter Half of the Eighteenth Century," *Bulletin of the John Rylands Library*, XLII (1959), 40-60; Arthur Redford, *Manchester Merchants and Foreign Trade, 1794-1858* (Manchester, 1934), pp. 1-14; Donald Read, *The English Provinces, c. 1760-1960* (London, 1964), p. 6.

[23] E. P. Thompson, *The Making of the English Working Class* (New York, 1964), p. 70; George Rudé, *Wilkes and Liberty; a Social Study of 1763 to 1774* (Oxford, 1962).

[24] R. B. Rose, "Eighteenth-Century Price Riots and Public Policy in England," *International Review of Social History*, VI (1961), 283-90.

ment, under pressure from manufacturing and mining districts, had been forced to permit free importation and prohibit exportation. No simple alignment in these matters existed between landowners and the rest of England. In their struggle against profiteers, rioters sometimes enlisted the sympathy of landowning magistrates hostile to traders, sometimes of magistrates more concerned with maintaining public order than the profits of food speculators, and occasionally of mineowners interested in keeping food prices low and the coal fields peaceful.[25]

The working classes as a political force made themselves felt in other ways during these years, apart from the price and availability of food. In 1765 machine-smashing riots won for miners the freedom to choose their own employers at the end of the annual contract. Belgian-woolen workers were strong enough in the 1760's to win collective agreements. And the successful frame-breaking activities of the East Midland hosiery trade had equally profound repercussions. Between 1776 and 1778, stocking-makers of the Midlands and London for the first time combined to form an effective organization and petitioned Parliament as one body for a bill to regulate wages. Though still embryonic, labor interests such as these were able to find M.P.'s to present their remonstrances and even elect sympathetic Members. Public fear, hostility, and rioting caused North's government to restrict the 1778 bill for relief of Roman Catholics to England, and not extend it to Scotland. As spokesman for the Scottish Protestant Association, Lord George Gordon fumed against any liberalization toward Roman Catholics, presented petitions to the Crown, and initiated a groundswell of popular opinion and agitation.[26]

The Church of England regained political strength and influ-

---

[25] *Ibid.*, pp. 290-92; see also S. G. E. Lythe, "The Tayside Meal Mobs, 1772-3," *Scottish Historical Review*, XLVI (1967), 26-36.

[26] Eric Hobsbawm, "The Machine-breakers," *Past and Present*, I (1952), 57-70; Jonathan D. Chambers, "The Worshipful Company of Framework Knitters (1657-1778)," *Economica*, IX (1929), 324-29; Christopher Hibbert, *King Mob: The Story of Lord George Gordon and the London Riots of 1780* (New York, 1958), pp. 40-42.

ence during the later 1760's and 1770's, as did the dissenting interest. Even the wigmakers strengthened their lobby in 1765 in order to petition for royal help; men of all stations caused increasing distress by wearing their own hair![27] Still more remarkable, however, was the ability of certain conscientious and industrious individuals in this era to bring pressure to bear on public bodies and institutions at the highest levels. Jonas Hanway, whose tracts against the "Jew bill" in 1753 helped to bring about its repeal, succeeded as a one-man lobby in getting an act in 1767 improving conditions in workhouses, freeing youths at the age of twenty-one, and obliging masters to feed and clothe their servants. Granville Sharp's single-minded, single-handed campaign to free Negro slaves in England began in 1765 and succeeded against staggering odds in 1772.[28]

Amidst all these diverse groups and individuals seeking to shape public policy through direct influence, the most active, controversial, problematic, and characteristic of the age were the various manufacturers. Their quickening political consciousness above all others made the two decades after 1763 a new and properly regarded "age of interests." When Samuel Garbett, a tough-minded industrialist, began to agitate for political cohesion among the manufacturers during the 1760's, lobbying techniques were haphazard and ineffective. Manufacturers were not yet prepared to think consistently in terms of collective action. Emphasis upon local issues and the tradition of reconciling local interests stood as obstacles to national or regional organization. Nevertheless, the Free Port Act of 1766 reflected the ambitions and pressures of British mercantile and manufacturing interests in developing Caribbean markets.

---

[27] Lewis B. Namier, *England in the Age of the American Revolution* (2nd ed.; London, 1961), p. 259; Norman Sykes, *Church and State in England in the Eighteenth Century* (Cambridge, Eng., 1934), chap. 7; Carl Bridenbaugh, *Mitre and Sceptre: Transatlantic Faiths, Ideas, Personalities, and Politics, 1689-1775* (New York, 1962), p. 287; B. S. Allen, *Tides in English Taste* (Cambridge, Mass., 1937), II, 184.

[28] John H. Hutchins, *Jonas Hanway, 1712-1786* (London, 1940), pp. 69, 75, 178, 185; E. C. P. Lascelles, *Granville Sharp and the Freedom of Slaves in England* (Oxford, 1928), chap. 4.

To secure sanctions in 1766 for the vital Trent-Mersey Canal, Garbett and Josiah Wedgwood organized a promotional campaign to shape landlord opinion in Parliament about the importance of canals, and to overcome the hostility of proprietors of existing river navigation systems and that of landowners through whose property the canal would be dug. Wedgwood prepared weekly articles for the London and provincial presses in support of the project.[29]

As a consequence of these activities, Wedgwood and Garbett first formed the idea of a national association, representing all industries, to educate politicians and unite manufacturers. A Manchester Committee for the Protection and Encouragement of Trade was formed in 1774 (reorganized in 1781). Then Garbett, with Matthew Boulton, established a Birmingham Commercial Committee. Similar bodies quickly followed at Halifax, Leeds, Exeter, and elsewhere; all intended to promote manufacturing interests by shaping the government's economic policies. At this time Garbett even used his considerable influence with governmental figures to promote the Carron iron works by having a law enforced to prevent workers from leaving England with trade secrets.[30]

This burst of organizational enthusiasm during the 1770's was symptomatic of intensive activity by smaller units at that time. In 1773 the vigorous silk manufacturers achieved their

---

[29] John M. Norris, "Samuel Garbett and the Early Development of Industrial Lobbying in Great Britain," *Economic History Review*, 2nd ser., X (1958), 450-51; Frances Armytage, *The Free Port System in the British West Indies: A Study in Commercial Policy, 1766-1822* (London, 1953), chap. 5; Read, *The English Provinces*, p. 25. The location of a canal in Scotland also elicited fierce competition among interests there in the 1760's. The enterprise required tremendous resources, stimulated the Board of Trustees for Fisheries and Manufactures, and led to strong competition for political power between Glasgow and Edinburgh (R. H. Campbell, *Scotland Since 1707: The Rise of an Industrial Society* [Oxford, 1965], pp. 48-49).

[30] Read, *The English Provinces*, pp. 25-26; Redford, *Manchester Merchants*, pp. 1-14; John Norris, "The Struggle for Carron: Samuel Garbett and Charles Gascoigne," *Scottish Historical Review*, XXXVII (1958), 136-45.

ultimate objective of strict prohibition against "importing and wearing of all foreign-wrought silk." When Sir Richard Arkwright and his associates mechanized the cotton industry, they encountered tremendous legal barriers, most of them designed to encourage the use of woolens and linens. In 1774 Arkwright and his Nottingham Company, "spinners of cotton stuffs," petitioned Parliament for relief. Basing their claims on the value of their new methods and the extent of their enterprises, they convinced Parliament of the need for legal redress. The House of Commons passed resolutions approving the new industry and declaring that prohibitions ought to be removed. The necessary legislation soon followed, permitting Englishmen to wear goods made entirely of cotton, and reducing the tax on textiles mixed with cotton by 50 per cent. By 1775 cotton manufacturing interests threatened the East Indian cotton trade as well as the wool industry. In 1780, despite protests from shipowners and West Indian interests, Manchester's Committee even gained some relief through permission to import cotton in neutral ships.[31]

In brief, a powerful wave of deliberate protective legislation swelled between 1763 and 1776, following forty years of more random flow in this direction. Protectionism meant many new prohibitions on imports: foreign silks, leather gloves, stockings, velvets, silk goods, linens, and some kinds of paper. Simultaneously duties were reduced on a whole range of needed raw materials, such as beaver skins and raw silk; and the export of textile machinery and tools was prohibited in 1774. Not surprisingly the "moneyed interest" grew apace during these years when trade and industry were rapidly extended. Between 1769 and 1772 thirteen new banking partnerships were created—a major addition to England's banking struc-

---

[31] Frank Warner, *The Silk Industry of the United Kingdom: Its Origin and Development* (London, [1921?]), pp. 181, 492; Witt Bowden, "The Influence of the Manufacturers on Some of the Early Policies of William Pitt," *American Historical Review*, XXIX (1924), 655; Redford, *Manchester Merchants*, p. 4.

ture.[32]   Technological developments in these years also
spawned new lobbies seeking favor in London. Matthew Boulton and James Watt organized an extraordinary campaign to
push through Parliament an extension to Watt's patent for an
improved steam engine. Boulton's broad interest in public
affairs, his involvement in the fashion trades, and, most of all,
his powerful social connections were tremendous assets in his
parliamentary endeavors.[33]

The years between the two peaces of Paris, then, did not
constitute an age of interests in the sense that special groups
controlled government, for that was not always possible or
desirable. Many of the groups themselves were unstable or
weak. Yet the peculiar essence of public life revealed governmental and general political absorption in the affairs of these
groups. The whole decision-making process was intimately tied
to concerns of special interests, and the major events of these
years were directed by the needs of, or crises created by, leading interest groups. Observers, both foreign and British, stand
as witnesses to this trend. During the 1760's and 1770's, for
example, liberal French intellectuals painted their picture of a
virtuous republic. For enlightened men like Mably, Holbach,
Diderot, and Rousseau, that republic left no room for conflicting interests. England, in their view, had fallen victim to
such interests and could never achieve the good society.[34]

THE RESPONSE: RHETORIC, RATIONALIZATION,
AND CRITICISM

In Britain a broad range of observers brought their notions of
political behavior into consonance with this reality. Hence the
recognition by the Scottish historical school "that a com-

[32] Ralph Davis, "The Rise of Protection in England, 1689-1786," *Eco-
nomic History Review*, 2nd ser., XIX (1966), 314; D. M. Joslin, "London
Private Bankers, 1720-1785," *ibid.*, VII (1954), 173.
[33] Eric Robinson, "Matthew Boulton and the Art of Parliamentary
Lobbying," *Historical Journal*, VII (1964), 209-29; see also B. D. Bargar,
"Matthew Boulton and the Birmingham Petition of 1775," *William and
Mary Quarterly*, 3rd ser., XIII (1956), 26-39.
[34] Frances Acomb, *Anglophobia in France, 1763-1789: An Essay in the
History of Constitutionalism and Nationalism* (Durham, 1950), pp. 37-38.

mercial organization of society had rendered obsolete much that had been believed about society before it."[35] Hence Sir William Mildmay's quest for a special department of commerce: "These difficulties in guiding *the separate interest of each Trade* to the general interest of the Whole, make it necessary for a government to appoint a particular department . . . to superintend the affairs of commerce, and examine all proposals. . . ."[36]

During the 1760's, theories of parliamentary representation became intertwined with the excess of interests. James Burgh and several other radicals wished for more merchants in the House of Commons because of their vital political importance. Josiah Tucker wondered in 1766 how colonies could complain about not being represented when so many interests, many of greater importance, were also unrepresented. Tucker would not accept the view that public and private interests necessarily harmonized. They often conflicted, he observed; government, therefore, must regulate interest groups in the general welfare.[37] Lord North, who disliked pressure groups and their agents, came to believe by 1779 that "the people of England collectively could only be heard [through] their representatives in Parliament."[38]

[35] J. G. A. Pocock, "Machiavelli, Harrington, and English Political Ideologies in the Eighteenth Century," *William and Mary Quarterly*, 3rd ser., XXII (1965), 582; Adam Ferguson, *An Essay on the History of Civil Society, 1767*, ed. Duncan Forbes (Edinburgh, 1966), esp. pp. 96-107.

[36] Mildmay, *The Laws and Policy of England, Relating to Trade* (London, 1765), p. 101. Italics mine.

[37] Wilfrid Harrison, *Conflict and Compromise: History of British Political Thought, 1593-1900* (New York, 1965), pp. 124-25; Josiah Tucker, *A Letter from a Merchant in London to His NEPHEW in AMERICA* (1766), in Robert L. Schuyler, ed., *Josiah Tucker: A Selection from His Economic and Political Writings* (New York, 1931), p. 311; Robert L. Schuyler, *The Fall of the Old Colonial System. . . .* (New York, 1945), p. 40.

[38] In December, 1772, North remarked to Samuel Martin that "a day spent in discussion in the country was worth fifty visits in Downing Street, where a dozen impatient gentlemen would be waiting in the ante-chamber, and he was liable to interruption at every moment." (See Eric Robson, "Lord North," *History Today*, II [1952], 537.) Samuel H. Beer, *British Politics in the Collectivist Age* (New York, 1965), p. 16.

When first elected an M.P. in 1765, Edmund Burke found it necessary to distinguish and analyze the various British and imperial interests. His sensitivity to their importance grew in succeeding years, so that by 1770 he argued against any man's achieving public office without first gaining experience and distinction among the major interests; otherwise, "such a man *has no connection with the interest of the people.*"[39] In addition to established groups of economic or commercial orientation, he noted that "a great official, a great professional, a great military and naval interest, all necessarily comprehending many people of the first weight, ability, wealth, and spirit, has been gradually formed in the kingdom . . . [and] must be let into a share of representation. . . ." While recognizing that the structure of British society was closely rooted in these diverse interests, Burke nevertheless believed that Parliament must not be regarded as a microcosm of them. Speaking in 1774, he offered his most extended thoughts on the place of interest groups in public life:

> Parliament is not a *congress* of ambassadors from different and hostile interests, which interests each must maintain, as an agent and advocate, against other agents and advocates; but Parliament is a *deliberative* assembly of *one* nation, with *one* interest, that of the whole—where not local purposes, not local prejudices, ought to guide, but the general good, resulting from the general reason of the whole. . . . We are now members for a rich commercial *city* [Bristol]; this city, however, is but a part of a rich commercial *nation*, the interests of which are various, multiform and intricate. We are members for that great nation, which however, is itself but a part of a great *empire*, extended by our virtue and our fortune to the farthest limits of the East and of the West. All these wide-spread interests must be considered,—must be compared,—must be reconciled, if possible.[40]

---

[39] Charles R. Fay, *Burke and Adam Smith* (Belfast, 1956), p. 14; Burke, *Thoughts on the Cause of the Present Discontents* (1770), in *The Works of Burke* (London, 1899), I, 473-74. Italics are Burke's.

[40] Gipson, *British Empire Before the Revolution*, XI, 203; Burke, *Speech to the Electors of Bristol . . . 3 November, 1774*, in *The Works of Burke*, II, 96-97. Italics are Burke's.

Men of other political complexions and allegiances joined Burke in recognizing that theirs was an Age of Interests. Their perspectives differed, however. Lord George Germain, shortly Secretary of State for the American Department, rose in 1774 to inform his peers that he "would not have men of a mercantile cast every day collecting themselves together, and debating about political matters; I would have them follow their occupations as merchants, and not consider themselves as ministers of that country." Similarly, Germain wished that the "tumultuous and riotous rabble" would "not trouble themselves with politics and government, which they do not understand."[41]

For Adam Smith, writing at the very same time, interest groups, especially merchants and manufacturers, exerted a truly pernicious influence. He did not believe in a comprehensive sort of natural harmony, as *The Wealth of Nations* and *Theory of Moral Sentiments* reveal. Although he thought landed and laboring interests were "inseparably connected with the general interest of the society," that of the commercial elements was "always in some respects different from, and even opposite to, that of the public." The older proposition that the state should intervene in economic life to reconcile conflicting interests of different groups rested on the belief that the state was *capable* of acting in the general interest, detached from pressures of special pleaders. Having by 1776 watched the ineffectual character of British government for nearly two decades, Smith had little faith in this idea. He had become convinced that legislative deliberations were often directed "by the clamorous importunity of partial interests."[42]

A recurrent theme in *The Wealth of Nations* laments the insidious influence of interest groups, especially in extorting monopolistic privileges from Parliament. Smith singled out woolen manufacturers as a group dangerously successful "in

---

41 *Parliamentary History of England*, XVII, 1195-96.
42 G. S. L. Tucker, *Progress and Profits in British Economic Thought, 1650-1850* (Cambridge, Eng., 1960), pp. 68-70; William Letwin, *The Origins of Scientific Economics* (New York, 1964), pp. 242-43.

persuading the legislature that the prosperity of the nation depended upon the success and extension of their particular business." The result, in this case as in so many others, was a vast array of corporation laws, duties, bounties, prohibitions, drawbacks, commercial treaties, and colonial monopolies.[43] The ultimate implication of interest-group activity, particularly as it concerned the American colonies, reached its denouement just before Smith published *The Wealth of Nations*. The crisis of Anglo-American relations was deeply rooted in the fierce competition among interest groups that characterized the 1760's and 1770's.

---

[43] *An Inquiry into the Nature and Causes of the Wealth of Nations*, ed. Edwin Cannan (London, 1950), I, 3, 129, 400, 435-36, 438; II, 18, 85, 114, 142, 146.

THE NORTH AMERICAN INTEREST
AND THE IMPERIAL CRISIS

IMPERIAL POLICY AND COLONIAL PETULANCE

Historians have long debated whether British colonial policy after 1763 shifted from mercantilism to imperialism. This should not have been an issue at all because real alterations occurred—regardless of their labels—and because the importance of 1763 as the pivotal year has perhaps been overemphasized. Changes in imperial policy had been in process for several generations. From 1715 to 1725 almost all the controversial measures enacted between 1763 and 1767 were discussed. These measures ranged from strengthening the Admiralty Courts to extending the stamp duties to America and using a molasses tax to raise revenue. Moreover, as early as 1754, Charles Townshend had formulated his infamous program for colonial reform. In 1767 he simply "carried into effect the scheme which he had put forward as a very junior minister in 1753-1754: a steadiness of purpose with which he has not been credited."[1]

---

[1] Thomas C. Barrow, *Trade and Empire: The British Customs Service in Colonial America, 1660-1775* (Cambridge, Mass., 1967), pp. 254-55; Lewis B. Namier, *Charles Townshend: His Character and Career* (Cambridge, Eng., 1959), p. 29.

The distinction between mercantilism and fiscality is quite relevant here. Mercantilism has been defined as the economic and political manifestation of statism, wherein doctrines are less important than the major goal of state-building. Fiscal questions concerning public revenue were independently considered, but always related to overall national purposes. Under fiscality, however, the nonfiscal implications of state policy were subordinated to the interests of the Treasury. From 1660 to 1775, fiscal-mindedness increased and more and more dominated governmental circles. In tobacco regulation, for example, the government conceded a rebate to encourage re-exportation; other than that it became less trade-oriented and more revenue-minded in its treatment of the tobacco trade. Laws curbing adulteration and use of damaged leaves in making smoking tobacco were designed primarily to protect the Treasury.[2]

Because of increasing imperial emphasis upon making colonies pay, the customs service assumed special importance after 1673, and especially after 1710, as an agency of enforcement. Not surprisingly, the politics of mercantilism was fought out in America, as well as in London, between provincials and imperial bureaucrats. The central theme in the story of the customs service, as its historian has noted, was its total inadequacy for the assignment with which it was entrusted. The early years—from 1673 to the rise of Walpole—were marked by a stubborn and general resistance by colonists to the work of customs officers. "In some colonies opposition reached from the office of the governor down to the smallest of the local courts. In others, the legislatures were the center of resistance. In all the colonies merchants and businessmen generally were

[2] Jacob M. Price, "The Tobacco Trade and the Treasury, 1685-1733: British Mercantilism in Its Fiscal Aspects" (Ph.D. dissertation, Harvard University, 1954); Barrow, *Trade and Empire,* also supports this emphasis upon a steady trend toward raising a revenue through the colonial customs service.

irritated at the restrictions on their activities and lent their support to efforts to emasculate the trade laws."[3]

Through legal obstructions, physical violence, and threats, the eighteenth-century colonists prevented customs officials from enforcing the Navigation Acts. Britain simply could not control the Americans' economic life without also supervising their political existence. As Professor Osgood put it many years ago, the mercantile system required "the existence of a high degree of both political and social unity as the condition of its success."[4] From 1720 until 1760 the colonies were left to develop very much on their own; they had little reason to complain of England's officiousness. The Molasses Act of 1733, theoretically prohibiting trade with non-British Caribbean islands, was not effectively enforced, as was often so characteristic of imperial policy during those years.[5]

The colonies benefited, in one sense, and were victimized in another, by vagaries of British imperial patronage. In 1758 an American wrote that English politicians "have been so careless for many years past of the characters and abilities of the civil officers appointed for America, that most of the places in the gift of the Crown have been filled with broken members of Par---t, of bad, if any principles, pimps, valet de chambres, electioneering scoundrels, and even livery servants. In one word, America has been for many years made the hospital of Great Britain for her decayed courtiers and abandoned worn-out dependents."[6] English colonial administration at mid-century was inefficiently organized and formed to an unhealthy degree by decisions of political patronage. It was also characterized by dangerous feuds between rival members of the imperial bureaucracy. Their bitter rivalries had occurred hap-

---

[3] Barrow, *Trade and Empire*, p. 253.

[4] Herbert L. Osgood, *The American Colonies in the Seventeenth Century* (New York, 1904), III, 241.

[5] Barrow, *Trade and Empire*, pp. 254-55.

[6] Ellis Huske, quoted in Massachusetts Historical Society *Collections*, 6th ser., VI (Boston, 1893), 3n.

hazardly during the first half of the century, but in the 1760's and 1770's, they would have a truly debilitating effect upon British authority and law enforcement in the colonies. In 1773, for example, Admiral John Montagu complained that his naval captains received no assistance from either customs officers or civil authorities.[7]

The imperial system that had evolved by the close of the Seven Years' War was "a composite of accidents, compromise, and unfulfilled projects." Careful, rational, and sensitive planning had long been needed, even more so after 1763. Such planning was not forthcoming, however, and new regulations provoked a prompt and hostile reaction in America. The Sugar (or Revenue) Act of 1764 left many problems unsolved, especially because of its failure to relieve imperial officials of their financial dependence on the colonists' funds and generosity. The Sugar Act was intended as the beginning of reform. But to antagonize American opposition without simultaneously strengthening the ability to enforce the government's program placed the program in jeopardy. Indeed, the very Empire itself was placed in jeopardy.

What became clear between 1764 and 1767 was the incompatibility of British administrative intentions with colonial commercial habits and aims. The colonists were determined to preserve the permissive circumstances which for decades had facilitated their economic growth. The British were equally determined by 1767-1768 to enforce their new policies through administrative reorganization. The American Board of Customs Commissioners was created in 1767 to bring "into execution the several laws relating to the revenues and trade of the said British colonies." Concurrently the Vice-Admiralty court system was reshuffled, with new courts established in 1768 at Boston, Philadelphia, and Charleston and a revitalized one at Halifax. These bodies had the same jurisdiction as provincial British Admiralty courts in cases concerning violations of trade

---

[7] Barrow, *Trade and Empire*, pp. 196-97, 236.

laws. Finally, also in 1768, a third Secretary of State was established—for an American Department. This decision might have been desirable in itself, because American affairs desperately needed centralized control and attention. But the first secretary appointed, Lord Hillsborough, was distinctly unsympathetic to colonial needs and aspirations. He became increasingly hostile and held office during the crucial years from 1768 until 1772.[8]

In essence, the program Charles Townshend offered Parliament in 1767 amounted to using funds raised in America to relieve royal officials there of any financial dependence on the colonists. All of the machinery for revenue collecting and enforcement would be tightened. In these respects, Townshend revitalized Grenville's earlier efforts. The goals of British policy in 1763 did not depart radically from Britain's "previous theory of empire. The departure was the attempt to enforce these goals. This is what caused Americans to reassess their place in the British empire." Grenville, for example, had begun serious use of the royal navy as an enforcement device; officers of war ships sent to America received Treasury warrants making them deputy custom officers.[9]

Yet by the fall of 1768 all these new measures had already revealed serious flaws and aroused a mounting opposition, especially in New England. Centralizing the customs service in an American Board simply accentuated colonial discontent and alienation. "The Commissioners came to symbolize the existence of an arbitrary external authority, and every successful attack on the Board or its members took on the aspect of a major colonial victory. Rather belatedly, the Treasury realized this point and cautioned the Commissioners to remember the delicate nature of their situation." Moreover the shortcomings

---

[8] Carl Ubbelohde, *The Vice-Admiralty Courts and the American Revolution* (Chapel Hill, N. C., 1960), pp. 128-47; Michael G. Kammen, *A Rope of Sand. The Colonial Agents, British Politics and the American Revolution* (Ithaca, N. Y., 1968), chaps. 12-13.

[9] Neil R. Stout, "Goals and Enforcement of British Colonial Policy, 1763-1775," *The American Neptune*, XXVII (1967), 220.

of the American Board typified how drastically Townshend had miscalculated. Townshend intended to increase the effectiveness of royal government in America. But Townshend's scheme touched upon the most delicate and sensitive areas in Anglo-American politics and trade. In so doing, it evoked a vituperative response in America and helped to solidify colonial opposition.[10]

After 1769 Lord North sought anxiously to protect England's constitutional and commercial supremacy as well as America's allegiance to the Empire. Early in 1770 he helped to gain parliamentary repeal of all Townshend Duties—except that on tea. Sensibly, he tried to avoid spurring American radicalism with the passage of inflammatory legislation. North simply hoped the knotty problems of Anglo-American relations could be overcome if ignored. At the very least, the American incendiaries would lapse into quiescence.

During the relatively calm years of 1770-1773, provincial discontent was primarily directed at the colonial customs service. Its officials, epitomizing the hated laws and policies of the 1760's, inevitably became targets for those committed to unqualified provincial autonomy. The Commissioners were described as "so many BLOOD SUCKERS UPON OUR TRADE."[11] Because they were expected to produce an imperial revenue at a time of extreme instability, their task was awkward in the extreme. Surprisingly they succeeded well in raising a considerable revenue, but not so well in avoiding political quicksand. Beginning with the Boston Massacre in March, 1770, numerous incidents further alienated American radicals and extended their search for searing indictments of crown and Parliament. The situation was reminiscent of a conversation once overheard on an airplane: "My daughter and her fiancé are having a slight difference." "Oh, really?" "Yes. She wants a large wedding, and he wants to break the engagement."

---

[10] Barrow, *Trade and Empire*, pp. 235, 240-42.

[11] Quoted in John C. Miller, *Origins of the American Revolution* (Stanford, Calif., 1959), p. 267.

"THE TENNIS BALL OF FACTION"

By 1769-1770 a combination of political, ideological, and economic circumstances had thrust a wedge into the imperial structure. British trade had recently found numerous new markets on the continent and in the East. Consequently, British merchants (and therefore the politicians) were simply less sensitive to pressure from their colonial correspondents. In April, 1770, William Strahan, a friend of Franklin's, wrote that "exports from this country to America in general are not at all, or but very little diminished; at least, not so far as to be anywhere, or among any Species of Manufacturers, sensibly felt. Had that been the Case, in this Petitioning and Remonstrating Age, we should have had Shoals of Complaints to Parliament from all Quarters." Moreover, "the *Silence* of *all* our Manufacturers, is *Demonstration itself*" that they were suffering no great hardship. In July he added that "Stagnation of our Trade to the Colonies makes no sensible Difference to the British Manufacturers. They either find other Markets for their Goods, from whence they are transmitted to you; or else they are smuggled in upon you."[12]

These conditions were complicated by the continued instability of English politics, a circumstance which made the colonial question merely a weapon in political infighting, rather than an object of statesmanship. As Edmund Burke remarked to the House of Commons in 1769, "I never thought America should be beat backwards and forwards, as the tennis ball of faction."[13]

By the close of the 1760's the shifting nature of English political society plainly required an overhauling of traditional ways of viewing government and public affairs. Burke himself was already moving toward a concept of "interest representa-

---

[12] "Letters of William Strahan, Printer," *Pennsylvania Magazine of History and Biography*, LX (1936), 477, 483.

[13] Elliott R. Barkan, ed., *Edmund Burke On the American Revolution: Selected Speeches and Letters* (New York, 1966), p. 6.

tion," a concept much closer to reality than the anachronistic language of government by "estates." Other Britons quickly saw that "interest representation" could be turned around and used against its creators. If conservatives could show that, despite the archaic system of representation, all major interests of the nation were virtually included in Parliament, then clearly there was no need for reform. The relation between interests and government thereby became a major constitutional issue, and even became linked with the problem of American (non-) representation in the imperial framework.[14]

British landed society changed significantly during the later eighteenth century. The heavy financial burden of three long wars placed enormous strains on weaker, less efficient, or less prosperous landowners. Meanwhile, men of new commercial wealth gained what appeared to be disproportionate political power, alarming members of the landed classes active in Parliament. This resulted in a continuum of sharp conflicts in the Commons. It also resulted in exposing the very concept of a landed interest as a peculiar ambiguity, because what appeared to be a homogeneous group "concealed a variety of elements, sometimes in harmony but sometimes in vital conflict." Similarly, commercial and industrial interests, many quite satisfied with their influence by the 1760's, lacked the unity suggested by their common designations. Much of their rivalry, however, emerged from fierce competition for government contracts, thereby accentuating how closely they were indeed connected by a similarity of interests.[15]

One of the most important political problems of the 1760's involved the future and fate of the East India Company. So crucial indeed was the matter to His Majesty's government that the complicated accommodation of 1766-1767 established a permanent government interest in the profits of the Company.

---

[14] J. R. Pole, *Political Representation in England and the Origins of the American Republic* (London, 1966), pp. 442-45.

[15] *Ibid.*, pp. 448-51.

Six years later, following reforms in the Company's organization, its management became a normal ministerial function. From the American colonial point of view, as J. R. Pole has observed, it must have "appeared a decisive comment on the meaning of 'virtual representation' that in 1773 the North Administration felt obliged to save the Company by granting it a monopoly of tea distribution in the colonies, without so much as pausing to discover whether the Colonies might have a different view."[16]

Even more conservative colonists, such as Governor Thomas Hutchinson of Massachusetts Bay, were deeply troubled by their decided disadvantage in what had, in many respects, become a system of interest representation. "Not one tenth part of the people of Great Britain," Hutchinson wrote, "have a voice in the elections to Parliament; and therefore, the colonies can have no claim to it; but every man of property in England may have his voice, if he will. Besides, acts of Parliament do not generally affect individuals, and every interest is represented. But the colonies have an interest distinct from the interest of the nation; and shall the Parliament be at once party and judge?"[17]

One very serious problem lay in Hutchinson's assumption that the colonies comprised a separate interest. They shared many common needs, and fears, to be sure. Moreover, contemporaries would indeed speak repeatedly of "the American interest." But there rarely existed the unity, cooperation, singleness of purpose, and leverage that would elicit a consistently positive response from ministers and Parliament. The most striking trend in imperial affairs during the decade after 1766 was perhaps the increasing inability of the American colonies to compete effectively in the politics of interest, imperialism, and mercantilism.

---

16 *Ibid.*, p. 450.

17 Quoted in Carl L. Becker, *The Declaration of Independence* (New York, 1922), p. 84.

THE AMERICAN INTEREST: ISOLATION AND IMPOTENCE

Adam Smith and Josiah Tucker, the two most prominent political economists of their generation, disagreed vigorously on many important issues, but on one major problem they concurred: that the origins of the American Revolution were entwined with the competition among British and colonial interests. How could one hope to "unite the most distant Situations, reconcile the most jarring Interests, the most opposite Principles, and discordant Tempers," asked Tucker? Although he envisioned subordination of North America's interests, Smith lamented that too much enforced subservience had created the dreadful impasse. "Of the greater part of the regulations concerning the colony trade," he wrote, "the merchants who carry it on . . . have been the principal advisers. We must not wonder, therefore, if, in the greater part of them, their interest has been more considered than either that of the colonies or that of the mother country . . . the interest of the colonies was sacrificed to the interest of those merchants." Before 1763 "the interest of our American colonies was regarded as the same with that of the mother country." Since then, however, a process of fragmentation and discrimination had occurred, distributing the economic burdens of empire unequally. In search of responsibility for these changes, Smith by-passed the politicians, believing instead that "merchants and manufacturers have been by far the principal architects."[18]

Smith's sentiments mirrored a mounting concern of the colonists ever since 1764, when the Sugar Act "was procured by the interest of the West India planters, with no other view than to enrich themselves, by obliging the northern Colonies to take their whole supply from them." In the middle colonies,

---

[18] Josiah Tucker, *The True Interest of Great Britain Set Forth in Regard to the Colonies* . . . (1774), in Schuyler, ed., *Josiah Tucker*, p. 339; Tucker, *A Letter to Edmund Burke, Esq.* . . . (1775), in *ibid.*, p. 394; Smith, *The Wealth of Nations*, II, 85, 146, 160.

as well as New England, observers noted that Americans "always looked with an evil eye on the West Indian interest as clashing with and opposing their own." To John Watts, a New York merchant, it seemed that "the West India and North American interest is always jarring." Even imperial bureaucrats in the colonies, such as Nathaniel Weare, Comptroller of Customs in Massachusetts, felt "there is not a man on the continent of America, who does not consider the Sugar Act . . . as a sacrifice made of the northern Colonies, to the superior interest in Parliament of the West Indies. . . . how the apprehension of so imperious a preference, of one Colony to another, operates upon the affections of those northern people towards the mother country, may be easily imagined."[19]

By 1765 the sense of discrimination and alienation had become general. "The Statutes made to restrain the trade of the Continent in favour of the islands," wrote John Dickinson, "seem to tend rather towards promoting *partial* than *general*, interests." Daniel Dulany echoed these sentiments, for "the commercial interests of Great Britain are preferred to every other consideration. . . ." Americans in London became more explicit in blaming rival interests for the precarious political situation. "Most of our acts of Parliament," wrote Franklin, "for regulating [trade, manufacturers, and taxes] are, in my opinion, little better than political blunders, owing to ignorance of the science, or to the designs of crafty men, who mislead the legislature, proposing something under the specious appearance of public good, while the real aim is, to sacrifice that to their own private interest." Franklin came to feel that special pleaders infested British politics, so that men in London could

---

[19] "Statement of Trade and Fisheries of Massachusetts," in Connecticut Historical Society *Collections*, XVIII (Hartford, 1920), 271-72; *Letter Book of John Watts* . . ., New-York Historical Society *Collections for 1928*, LXI (New York, 1928), 388; Agnes M. Whitson, "The Outlook of the Continental American Colonies on the British West Indies, 1760-1775," *Political Science Quarterly*, XLV (1930), 69, 73, 76; Weare, "Observations on the British Colonies on the Continent of America," Massachusetts Historical Society *Collections*, 1st ser., I (Boston, 1792), 83-84.

have no understanding of political behavior based upon principles. "They have no Idea that any People act from any other Principle but that of Interest; and they believe, that 3 d. in a lb. of Tea . . . is sufficient to overcome all the Patriotism of an American."[20]

Hopeful assumptions and expectations developed by colonists before and during the Seven Years' War were clouded over after 1763, leading them to wonder about the relative efficacy of the North American interest in London.[21] During the war, for example, Britain's temporary possession of a number of the French West Indies had led to the exportation of large quantities of rice from South Carolina to these islands. Because rice was an enumerated commodity, however, this trade became illegal in 1763 on the return of Martinique and Guadeloupe to France, leading to an anxious series of parliamentary petitions from South Carolina and Georgia. Early in 1765 Franklin revealed to American correspondents his fear that the Stamp Act would pass "notwithstanding all the Opposition that could be given it by the American Interest." Franklin's habit, he believed, had always been to consider the welfare of the whole society or community. Thus, his first economic pamphlet in 1729 had concerned the "true Interest" of Pennsylvania, and his great imperial essay of 1760 considered *The Interest of Great Britain . . . With Regard to Her Colonies.* By the middle and later sixties, however, he saw the

---

[20] [John Dickinson], *The Late Regulations Respecting the British Colonies on the Continent of America Considered* . . . (Philadelphia, 1765), in *The Political Writings of John Dickinson* (Wilmington, Del., 1801), I, 58-60; Dulany, *Considerations on the Propriety of Imposing Taxes in the British Colonies* (Annapolis, 1765), in Bernard Bailyn, ed., *Pamphlets of the American Revolution, 1750-1776* (Cambridge, Mass., 1965), I, 624; Franklin to Lord Kames, 1 Jan. 1769, Smyth, *Writings of Franklin*, V, 187; Franklin to Thomas Cushing, 4 June 1773, *ibid.*, VI, 57. In 1776 Carter Braxton of Virginia blamed British tyranny on "a monied interest" which had usurped the power of the crown (see *Pamphlets of the American Revolution*, I, 182-83).

[21] Gilman M. Ostrander, "The Colonial Molasses Trade," *Agricultural History*, XXX (1956), 84.

American interest as a discrete entity and worried that its London facade was beginning to crumble.[22]

His concerns were justified. Compared with its competitors the North American interest suffered from certain strategic disadvantages. There was the problem of distance. As James Roebuck, an authority on lobbying in Georgian England, noted, it was much easier speaking to members of Parliament than writing to them. Because of this fact, the task of presenting the colonial case fell largely to the agents, whereas the strength and leverage of other lobbies were more broadly based. To compound the difficulty, after 1768 the agents' role became highly ambiguous, while their employers became the only interest regarded unfavorably for intellectual and constitutional reasons. When Lord North announced that Parliament would "not consent to go into the question [of repealing the Townshend Duties], on account of the combinations going on in America against the mother country," he essentially declared that in an age of government sensitivity to group pressure, one group in particular was beyond the pale.[23]

Its isolation, moreover, was compounded by several factors. First, there was the loss of identification between colonial groups and their counterparts in Britain. What had once been trans-Atlantic interests became separated into distinct groups. Relations between merchants, dissenters, and shipbuilders on both sides of the ocean deteriorated.[24] Pitt had remarked to

[22] George Louis Beer, *British Colonial Policy, 1754-1765* (New York, 1907), p. 225; Franklin to David Hall, 14 Feb. 1765, Smyth, *Writings of Franklin*, IV, 363; Alfred O. Aldridge, *Benjamin Franklin: Philosopher and Man* (Philadelphia, 1965), pp. 139, 147, 171, 205.

[23] Robinson, "Boulton and the Art of Lobbying," p. 216; Gipson, *British Empire Before the Revolution*, XI, 243-44, 253. For Burke's caustic comments upon the effect of distance on the North American agents, see his speech, "On Conciliation," 22 March 1775, in Elliott R. Barkan, ed., *Edmund Burke on The American Revolution* (New York, 1966), pp. 115-16.

[24] Cf. Arthur H. Buffinton, "The Policy of Albany and English Western Expansion," *Mississippi Valley Historical Review*, VIII (1922), 361-62; Joseph J. Malone, *Pine Trees and Politics: The Naval Stores and Forest Policy in Colonial New England, 1691-1775* (Seattle, 1964), p. 43; Josiah Tucker, *Letter to Edmund Burke*, p. 382.

the House of Commons in 1759 "that he did not know but the landed gentlemen seemed to consider themselves in a separate interest from the colonies, that he should ever consider the colonies as [part of] the landed interest of this Kingdom and it was a barbarism to consider them otherwise." His remarks were not well received. By 1767 a major objection to colonial concessions was that "the landed interest of the colonies, will be promoted; while the . . . landed interest of Great Britain will be depressed to its utter ruin and destruction and, consequently, the balance of the power of government . . . will be *locally* transferred from Great Britain to the colonies." Franklin insisted that "the contrary had always been the fact," i.e., assistance to American agriculture had benefited the entire Empire.[25]

The isolation of North America's London interest increased despite the agent's protest, especially after 1766. Repeal of the Stamp Act had in part been possible because, as Richard Jackson, an agent for several colonies, observed: "however the Colonies have friends, I sh[oul]d say, the British Empire has friends." After 1769 it was no longer possible to "consider the Merchants here [Philadelphia] and in England as the Links of the Chain that binds both Countries together."[26] Bristol's Society of Merchant Venturers had petitioned for repeal in 1766. After 1770 it ceased to support the North American interest. The iron industry had also sought repeal, but in 1775 Birmingham's iron manufacturers hoped for stringent enforcement of Parliament's punitive colonial legislation. The prospect of war meant a tremendous boom for the industry. In petitioning against the Coercives during the spring of 1774, William

[25] Pares, *War and Trade in the West Indies*, p. 509; Thomas Pownall to Franklin, and Franklin's reply, in John Bigelow, ed., *The Complete Works of Benjamin Franklin* (New York, 1887), IV, 63-64. See also Burke's speech before the House of Commons, 13 Nov. 1770, excerpted in *Edmund Burke on the American Revolution*, p. 23.

[26] Jackson to Thomas Fitch, 15 Nov. 1765, Connecticut Historical Society *Collections*, XVIII, 376; Barrow, *Trade and Empire*, pp. 214-15; Arthur M. Schlesinger, *The Colonial Merchants and the American Revolution, 1763-1776* (2nd ed.; New York, 1957), p. 31.

Bollan, agent for the Massachusetts Council, "had considerable expectation that the honorable India merchants would assist and strengthen your defence; afterwards that the manufacturers in the principal towns, who, according to my information, were alarmed, and stirring, would make their opposition to the Bill for shutting up the port; but all failed, even the London merchants declining their opposition to it."[27]

Practically the only area in which the North American interest did not stand isolated involved the intellectual sympathies of English radicals; ironically, that trans-Atlantic connection would hasten rather than impede the imperial breach. In 1769 John Horne Tooke founded in London the Society of the Supporters of the Bill of Rights. The organization acquired a national reputation and generated enthusiasm in the colonies, where Sam Adams became an overseas member. His efforts led to creation of similar units which then helped stir revolutionary unrest in the early 1770's.[28]

Until the Stamp Act crisis, a coalition of agents, merchants, religious societies and such championed North American interests in London. By the later sixties the agents' supporting elements were partially dispersed, with group disintegration compounding their isolation.

On December 4, 1765, "the Merchants [of London] trading to North America" had formally organized as a lobby to assist the colonial interest. In alliance with provincial agents in 1766-1767, they would seek repeal of the Currency Act of 1764. In fact, many of the very same merchants instrumental in securing the Currency Act to protect their American investments now urged repeal as part of a general reform of colonial trade. Early in 1767, especially, the Committee of North

---

[27] Walter E. Minchinton, "The Stamp Act Crisis: Bristol and Virginia," *Virginia Magazine of History and Biography*, LXXIII (1965), 146-55; Pelham, "The West Midland Iron Industry," pp. 161-62; Gipson, *British Empire Before the Revolution*, XII, 122-23.

[28] Chilton Williamson, *American Suffrage from Property to Democracy, 1760-1860* (Princeton, 1960), pp. 71-73.

American merchants was activated to search for some viable accommodation with the agents. But the Committee was quickly alienated by intemperate action in America, notably New York where the Assembly refused to respect the Mutiny Act and petitioned against the Revenue Act of 1766. The alliance of London and Glasgow merchants with West Indian planters and traders had collapsed, leaving "a rump lobby of London merchants" whose political effectiveness in working for repeal of the Currency Act and other colonial reforms was much reduced.[29]

Before the mid-sixties, colonial land companies and their London lobbyists had not been incompatible with the colonial agents. In the eight years or so before independence, however, the increased tempo of land company politicking by Americans undermined the integrity and single-mindedness of the agents. Virginia and agent Edward Montagu were pitted against the Grand Ohio Company and Benjamin Franklin by 1770, while Arthur Lee and the Mississippi Company (a Virginia group) aroused the hostility of Pennsylvania's proprietors.[30] Competition between exponents of the land companies had always existed; but by 1769 a mad scramble was under way among the Ohio, Indiana, Mississippi, Grand Ohio, and Vandalia Companies to secure or obstruct vast grants of American real estate. In support of the Vandalia Company, Samuel Wharton single-handedly created a special lobby, whose executive committee included Thomas Walpole, Wharton, John Sargent, and Benjamin Franklin. Despite superb connections, however, the group failed to achieve its objectives. Its attempts between

---

[29] Joseph A. Ernst, "The Currency Act Repeal Movement: A Study of Imperial Politics and Revolutionary Crisis," *William and Mary Quarterly*, 3rd ser., XXV (1968), 185, 194-96, 210.

[30] Nicholas B. Wainwright, *George Croghan: Wilderness Diplomat* (Chapel Hill, N. C., 1959), chap. 10; Peter Marshall, "Lord Hillsborough, Samuel Wharton and the Ohio Grant, 1769-1775," *English Historical Review*, LXXX (1965), 722-23, 726, 735; Richard B. Morris, *The Peacemakers. The Great Powers and American Independence* (New York, 1965), p. 249.

1770 and 1775 did nothing to elevate the North American interest in British eyes.[31]

One response to its deterioration in London was an increase in political activity and organization in the New World. News of such events was not well received in England, where there was skepticism "of such mixt interests as the Colonys are compos'd of." Political consciousness quickened in Boston, New York, Philadelphia, and Charleston during these years, leading, for example, to formation in 1763 of the Society for Encouraging Trade and Commerce within the Province of Massachusetts Bay, and to New York's commercial groups.[32] In March, 1768, Daniel Malcolm, a "little trader" who had earlier made a reputation for himself by resisting customs officers, presided over a general meeting of Boston merchants called to discuss the newest British measures. As Governor Bernard suggested, this was really the first extra-legal assembly called in Boston in protest against the acts of Parliament. Yet compared with the impact of London and the outports on British politics at this time, colonial cities were a marginal force.[33] Southern colonial threats to manufacture their own products were not very effective as economic sanctions either, and only brought occasional concessions.[34]

---

[31] John Mercer to Charlton Palmer, 27 July 1762, in Lois Mulkearn, ed., *George Mercer Papers Relating to the Ohio Company of Virginia* (Pittsburgh, 1954), pp. 46-48; Sewall E. Slick, *William Trent and the West* (Harrisburg, Pa., 1947), chap. 11, pp. 139-54.

[32] Namier, *England in the Age of the American Revolution*, p. 262; Carl Bridenbaugh, *Cities in Revolt: Urban Life in America, 1743-1776* (New York, 1955); Charles M. Andrews, "The Boston Merchants and the Non-Importation Movement," Colonial Society of Massachusetts *Publications*, XIX (1918), 161-68; Virginia D. Harrington, *The New York Merchant on the Eve of the Revolution* (New York, 1935), pp. 173, 204, 244; Arthur L. Jensen, *The Maritime Commerce of Colonial Philadelphia* (Madison, Wisc., 1963); Leila Sellers, *Charleston Business on the Eve of the Revolution* (Chapel Hill, N. C., 1934).

[33] Barrow, *Trade and Empire*, pp. 228-29; Lucy S. Sutherland, *The City of London and the Opposition to Government, 1768-1774* (London, 1959).

[34] C. Robert Haywood, "Economic Sanctions: Use of the Threat of Manufacturing by the Southern Colonies," *Journal of Southern History*, XXV (1959), 207-19.

In sum, at a time when pressure groups constituted the matrix of politics, the North American interest was a relatively weak entity, especially within Parliament. As Isaac Barré commented, "there are gentlemen in this House from the West Indies, but there are very few who know the circumstances of North America."[35] Advocates of the mainland colonies were less well-connected and organized, less well-financed and informed, less committed and, in several cases, less capable than their rivals,[36] who knew what they sought, and how far they might go in achieving it. North America's political influence in no way equalled its economic importance. Too often the colonies were on the defensive because a more aggressive interest had taken the offensive against them. More and better agents, a more cohesive and purposeful lobby in London, and greater political use of economic leverage were required.

Instead the North American agents became less of an interest group and more a constitutional protagonist, thereby violating the political conventions of the age. In consequence the group's isolation and fragmentation—as well as its employers' alienation—encountered deep hostility from North's administration and from other interest groups as well. In 1767 Charles Townshend decided that endless complications would follow if the government pressed its "right" to certain East India Company revenues. Therefore, the sensible policy for the government involved an amicable arrangement with the Company, avoiding the question of right altogether. Similarly, Lord

---

[35] Esmond Wright, ed., *Causes and Consequences of the American Revolution* (Chicago, 1966), p. 212; Lewis B. Namier and John Brooke, *The History of Parliament: The House of Commons, 1754-1790* (London, 1964), I, 161. In 1769 Barré again chastised the House: "So full a House upon this occasion [the Wilkes affair] is an impeachment of parliament. Upon the American affairs you had not above half the number." John Wright, ed., *Sir Henry Cavendish's Debates of the House of Commons During the Thirteenth Parliament of Great Britain* (London, 1841-43), II, 126.

[36] See the discussion in Julian P. Boyd's introduction to *The Susquehanna Company Papers. Memorial Publications of the Wyoming Historical and Genealogical Society* (Wilkes-Barre, Pa., 1930-33), II, xi.

North might have reached an accommodation with the colonial agents just as he did with Thomas Allan, Ireland's agent, in the difficult and complicated circumstances of 1770-1771. The attitudes and pressures of the other major groups served as a preventive of sorts.[37]

Food and price riots, as well as machine-smashing in England, brought a modicum of redress to working classes there after 1766. In the colonies a tea party that also damaged private property brought rapid retribution. In direct clashes with the African interest over slave importations, North American agents came off badly, as they lamented to their friends at home.[38] As 1775 opened, the alignment was overwhelming. Provincial merchants and manufacturers were activated, as Matthew Boulton wrote, "to prevent, if possible, some of my neighbours from running into unwise measures, [initiated] by the intrigues of American and minority agents, who I have reason to believe have been busy . . . in most of the other manufacturing towns in England." Simultaneously, the fisheries interest welcomed the administration's program to restrict colonial trade and fishing opportunities.[39]

Edmund Burke summarized the impasse in January:

If the Merchants had thought fit to interfere last Winter [1773-1774], the distresses of this might certainly have been prevented; conciliatory Measures would have taken place; and they would have come with more dignity, and with far better effect, before the Trial of our Strength than after it. . . . By Means of this reserve, the authority of the Mercantile Interest,

---

[37] Gipson, *British Empire Before the American Revolution*, XI, 92-93. The well-known pamphlet by William Knox, *The Interests of the Merchants and Manufacturers of Great Britain* . . ., was inspired by North's ministry in 1774, seeking to shape mercantile opinion. See Jack M. Sosin, *Agents and Merchants. British Colonial Policy and the Origins of the American Revolution, 1763-1775* (Lincoln, Neb., 1965), pp. 219-20.

[38] William R. Riddell, "Pre-Revolutionary Pennsylvania and the Slave Trade," *Pennsylvania Magazine of History and Biography*, LII (1928), 18-19; Arthur Lee to Joseph Reed, 18 Feb. 1773, Reed MSS, New-York Historical Society.

[39] Bargar, "Boulton and the Birmingham Petition," p. 30; Clark, *British Opinion and the American Revolution*, p. 89.

which ought to have supported, with efficacy and power, the opposition to the fatal Cause of all this Mischief, was pleaded against us; *and we were obliged to stoop under the accumulated weight of all the Interests in this Kingdom. . . .*[40]

By September these conditions had only worsened. Stirrings on the part of a few British merchants for reconciliation were meaningless. The North American interest had ceased to exist; its transformation, however, inaugurated a new era.[41]

THE ULTIMATE RESPONSE: REVALUATION AND REVOLUTION

The intellectual evaluation of that era in the American mind was inextricably bound up with the history of the 1760's and 1770's. In 1774 Thomas Jefferson's *Summary View* observed that "the addition of new *states* to the British Empire has produced an addition of new, and sometimes opposite interests." The next year John Adams, as Novanglus, blamed the initial statutory problems of 1764 upon "the private interest of provincial governors and West India planters," along with "a few Portugal merchants." Speculating upon a reconstruction of Parliament, Adams observed that it would require "a House of Lords, consisting of Irish, East and West Indian, African, American, as well as English and Scottish noblemen."[42]

Nevertheless Americans did not blithely believe interests could be eradicated from political society. Late in 1775, Adams worried over curtailment of colonial commerce overseas. Could the Americans persevere? "Is not the Merchantile Inter-

---

[40] Burke to Richard Champion, [10] Jan. 1775, in George H. Guttridge, ed., *The Correspondence of Edmund Burke* (Chicago, 1961), III, 95-96. My italics.

[41] Rev. James Madison to St. George Tucker, 20 Sept. 1775, in Charles Crowe, "The Reverend James Madison in Williamsburg and London, 1768-1771," *West Virginia History*, XXV (1964), 275; Clark, *British Opinion and the American Revolution*, pp. 99-100.

[42] Richard W. Van Alstyne, *Empire and Independence: The International History of the American Revolution* (New York, 1965), p. 41; Charles F. Adams, ed., *The Works of John Adams* (Boston, 1850-56), IV, 49; Samuel Eliot Morison, ed., *Sources and Documents Illustrating the American Revolution, 1764-1788* (New York, 1965), p. 127.

est comprehending Merchants, Mechanicks, Labourers So numerous, and So complicated with the Landed Interest, as to produce a general Impatience and Uneasiness, under Restriction so severe?" In 1776 Adams published his *Thoughts on Government*, in which he discussed creation of the ideal representative assembly. It would be a microcosm of the people at large, wherein "equal interests among the people should have equal interests."[43]

That same year a highly original and prescient pamphlet appeared by an unknown author, entitled *Four Letters on Interesting Subjects*. He argued for a single legislative house because two houses would only embody two sets of conflicts among interests. Suppose "the landed interest would get into one house, and the commercial interest into the other." To avoid this the author wished for a single house, "and *that one* to consist of every sort" of interest. By 1776, the social basis of political thought was shifting. The essential units participating in the constitution, as Bernard Bailyn has shown, were no longer formal orders of society derived from the assumptions of an earlier era, but interests organized for political action, which became factions and parties. Embodied in the most advanced thinking in America "were the shifting, transitory competitive groupings into which men of the eighteenth century actually organized themselves in the search for wealth, prestige, and power."[44]

During the first half of the eighteenth century these groups, along with the formal political alignments and rate of economic growth, remained comparatively stable. After mid-century, however, a period of accelerated economic activity and simultaneous changes in the configuration of interest groups were

---

[43] Adams to James Warren, 20 Oct. 1775, in Edmund C. Burnett, ed., *Letters of Members of the Continental Congress* (Washington, 1921), I, 240; [Adams], *Thoughts on Government: Applicable to the Present State of the American Colonies*, in *Works*, IV, 195. In analyzing the importance of an independent judiciary, Adams observed that "their minds should not be distracted with jarring interests; they should not be dependent upon any man, or body of men." (*Ibid.*, p. 198.)

[44] *Pamphlets of the American Revolution*, I, 187-88.

quickly followed by a sustained period of political instability. Given the total picture of competitive demands upon the imperial government, the nature of the decision-making process then, and the limited "Seasons of business,"[45] the equilibrium of public life and imperial imperatives was at best precarious. Under these circumstances, the North American interest played the maverick's role; waning in influence, it became ideologically entangled. This was enough to upset the balance, for as Landon Carter of Virginia had cautioned in 1764, "any man who makes an *Idol of his Interest* must make a *Martyr* of his *Integrity*."

---

[45] J. Steven Watson has shown that between 1760 and 1775 there was so much business to be handled that Parliament was unable to function properly ("Parliamentary Procedure as a Key to the Understanding of Eighteenth-Century Politics," *Burke Newsletter,* III [1962], 107-28). See also Michael Kammen, "The American Colonies and the 'Seasons of Business' in Eighteenth-Century Britain," in *Anciens Pays et Assemblées D'Etats. Etudes Publiées par la Section Belge de la Commission Internationale Pour L'Histoire Des Assemblées D'Etats,* XLVIII (Brussels, 1970).

EPILOGUE. YET ANOTHER
TRANSFORMATION

REALIGNMENT IN BRITAIN AFTER 1783

During the War of American Independence, especially its closing years, the dominant role of interest groups in British and
imperial public life reached a plateau, then began levelling off.
Agitation for parliamentary reform reached a climax between
1779 and 1781, with the Yorkshire leadership stimulating new
and important kinds of extraparliamentary associations.[1] Ireland won the right of partial legislative autonomy in 1782, and
in that year a panoply of groups affected by the preliminary
peace negotiations stirred themselves into action. Canadian fur
merchants, fisheries men, Tobago planters, logwood merchants,
the East India Company, and American Loyalists all were
aroused to a frenzy of political activity that culminated in 1783.[2]

Thereafter British attitudes toward interest groups and the
relationship of interests to the government underwent a period
of adjustment. The interests remained active, with the politicians and ministers still consulting them. But, with the return
of political stability, government regained the initiative and

---

[1] Ian R. Christie, *Wilkes, Wyvill and Reform: the Parliamentary Reform
Movement in British Politics, 1760-1785* (London, 1962); Eugene C. Black,
*The Association: British Extraparliamentary Political Organization from
1769 to 1793* (Cambridge, Mass., 1963).

[2] Richard B. Morris, *The Peacemakers* (New York, 1965), pp. 418-19,
433, 547n125.

decisive control over policy. This was not at all obvious in 1784 and 1785, when British manufacturers reached a great peak in organization and influence. But beginning in 1786, their grand national alliance dwindled, as Pitt's administration firmly and determinedly seized the reins of power. "In the 1780's and '90's the older view prevailed, that affairs of state were the affairs of statesmen."[3]

During these years the African Company's influence lessened appreciably, especially in 1782 when the Board of Trade was abolished. The Hudson's Bay Company had to fight off a strong competitor in the North West Company. An axis of cooperation developed between the Merchants of Montreal and their London correspondents which diminished the Bay Company's power after 1783. The West Indian interest continued its slow decline in the 1780's, while the East India Company, despite a burst of activity in 1782-1784, thereafter ceased to affect politics as it had during the previous decade. The enactment of William Pitt's proposal in 1784 established a Court of Directors and Proprietors to be overseen by a governmental control board appointed by the crown. It thereby acquired supervision of the Company's political and military activities.[4]

Members and defenders of the commercial communities bemoaned the "sufferings of the mercantile interest" in these years, and tended to blame "this monied interest," to which great powers were attributed. Actually both groups were somewhat less powerful after 1783, while the Bank of England

[3] John Ehrman, *The British Government and Commercial Negotiations With Europe, 1783-1793* (Cambridge, Eng., 1962), pp. 32, 42-47, 54, 63-66, 183-85.

[4] Eveline C. Martin, *The British West African Settlements, 1750-1821* (London, 1927), p. 28; Wayne E. Stevens, "The Organization of the British Fur Trade, 1760-1800," *Mississippi Valley Historical Review*, III (1916), 201-202; Lowell J. Ragatz, *The Fall of the Planter Class in the British Caribbean, 1763-1833* (New York, 1928), pp. 144-69, 183; C. H. Philips, "The East India Company 'Interest' and the English Government, 1783-84," *Transactions of the Royal Historical Society*, 4th ser., XX (1937), 83-101.

was reduced in importance as a result of Pitt's quest for financial reform.[5] The City of London's political role also was lessened by comparison with its position during the 1750's, 1760's, and 1770's, and counterbalanced by the rise of the provinces to prominence in national politics. From the early 1780's, trading boroughs with seats in Parliament began to send local businessmen to the Commons instead of members of local landed families.[6]

The changing political sensitivity of new urban areas in the British provinces was closely tied to the development of manufacturing in those areas. By the 1780's Glasgow had numerous trade organizations and societies. Their vigor led in 1783 to establishment of the Glasgow Chamber of Commerce and Manufactures, one of the earliest such bodies to form. By that time, industrialists all over Britain were alert to the need for a greater and permanent voice in politics. Samuel Garbett, of Birmingham, and Josiah Wedgwood, leading figures in the national movement, saw their dreams materialize in 1785 with the founding of the General Chamber of Manufacturers. They had repeatedly pleaded with industrialists not to confine their loyalty to "associations of *single* and *detached* bodies of Merchants and Manufacturers"; but rather to support the movement for organization of "*the whole manufacturing Interest of the Island.*"[7]

The origin of the General Chamber can be traced easily to

---

[5] Richard Champion, *Comparative Reflections on the Past and Present Political, Commercial, and Civil State of Great Britain* ... (London, 1787), pp. 28-29, 264, 320; Sir John Clapham, *The Bank of England: A History* (New York, 1945), I, 173-99.

[6] Lucy Sutherland, "The City of London in Eighteenth-Century Politics," in Richard Pares and A. J. P. Taylor, eds., *Essays Presented to Sir Lewis Namier* (London, 1956), pp. 72-73; Donald Read, *The English Provinces c. 1760-1960* (London, 1964), p. 22.

[7] W. R. Scott, "Adam Smith and the Glasgow Merchants," *Economic Journal*, XLIV (1934), 506-508; Read, *The English Provinces*, p. 24; Arthur Redford, *Manchester Merchants and Foreign Trade* (Manchester, 1934), I, 9.

the hostility to Pitt's excise and Irish policies in 1784-1785. Cotton, iron, and pottery interests were thereby stimulated to unite with various groups of older petty manufacturers. Success in achieving repeal of the cotton tax in 1784 whetted their appetite for politics. Early the next year *The Plan of the General Chamber of Manufacturers of Great Britain* was published, claiming that "the *landed* and *funded interest*, the *East-India*, and other commercial bodies, have their respective advocates in the great council of the nation," while manufacturers alone lacked a national body to represent them. With establishment of a London headquarters in 1785, immediate victories were anticipated and achieved. Nevertheless, the General Chamber's national cohesion proved ephemeral. By 1786 weaknesses were apparent; splits developed along regional lines as well as between traditional trades and newer industries. Even local groups, such as Manchester's Committee for the Protection of Trade, became ineffectual because of internal diversity and bickering.[8]

By 1787 the General Chamber was foundering on disputes over the most effective indirect influence. Disagreement over the French Commercial Treaty destroyed the immature national body and scattered its component members back to their provincial strongholds. Whereas newer industries hoped for reciprocal trade agreements which would open new markets, older interests feared the competition which would accompany such agreements. Pitt, of course, welcomed the General Chamber's collapse. He had refused to deal with it as a body, though during negotiations with France he maintained contact with leading members as individuals. More than half a century would pass before manufacturers thought again in terms of a permanent, national organization. At that time

8 Witt Bowden, "The Influence of the Manufacturers on Some of the Early Policies of William Pitt," *American Historical Review*, XXIX (1964), 655-74; Read, *The English Provinces*, pp. 26-30, 33; Redford, *Manchester Merchants and Foreign Trade*, p. 13.

they would achieve their first decisive victory over the landed interest.[9]

The larger point to keep in mind is that the long attack on mercantilism in Britain gained sustaining momentum at the close of the American Revolutionary era. The economic structure of mercantilism endured for a half-century more. Mercantile thought, however, was more shortlived. By the mid-1780's, it was in retreat everywhere, except in America, where a form of neomercantilism guided the newly independent states, then searching for an understanding and regulation of their proper economic relationship to one another.[10]

READJUSTMENT IN ANGLO-AMERICA AFTER 1783

By the mid-1780's interest groups in America emerged to positions of considerable political significance, accompanied by the advanced continuation of an intellectual alteration we'l under way by 1776.[11] To John Adams "only laws made jointly by the representatives of all the interests in society could be trusted with unlimited confidence. They alone provided the bond which gave unity to a commonwealth." How else could one hope to reconcile the "diversity of sentiments, contradic-

---

[9] Witt Bowden, *Industrial Society in England Towards the End of the Eighteenth Century* (2nd ed.; London, 1965), pp. 181-93; Read, *The English Provinces*, p. 33; Michael Flinn, "The Industrialists," in Alex Natan, ed., *Silver Renaissance: Essays in Eighteenth-Century English History* (London, 1961), pp. 78-79.

[10] R. Coupland, *The American Revolution and the British Empire* (London, 1930), chap. 5, "The Attack on Mercanti'ism"; William A. Williams, "The Age Of Mercantilism: an Interpretation of the American Political Economy, 1763 to 1828," *William and Mary Quarterly*, 3rd ser., XV (1958), 419-37. Williams' suggestive and interesting interpretation must nevertheless be read with critical care.

[11] Paul Goodman, *The Democratic-Republicans of Massachusetts; Politics in a Young Republic* (Cambridge, Mass., 1964), pp. 6-10; Forrest McDonald, *We The People: The Economic Origins of the Constitution* (Chicago, 1958), chap. 9; William Smith, Jr., *Historical Memoirs . . .*, ed. William H. W. Sabine (New York, 1956-58), II, 306.

tory principles, inconsistent interests and opposite passions" which were everywhere so pressing?[12]

Benjamin Franklin was equally sensitive to the pattern of interest group politics. In Congress he hoped that interests of individual states would be subordinated to the common weal. Soon after the Philadelphia Convention in 1787 he wrote a French friend that experience had just shown the possibility of reconciling conflicting interest groups. The ratification struggle, however, quickly imposed a more realistic view. In politics the participants were many, "their ideas so different, their prejudices so strong and various, and their particular interests, independent of the general, seeming so opposite, that not a move can be made that is not contested." In Franklin's mature thinking, competition and wrangling among groups "tended to open sores in the body politic and drain it of energy which otherwise might be more constructively channeled." Hence his hope that when particular groups within the polity collided, they could be made to understand that the orbits of component units should be respected in the greater interest of communal and national harmony.[13]

Like Adams and Franklin in the 1780's, James Madison was moving away from the politics of interest, through the politics of revolutionary ideology, to that of social harmony and balance. Interest groups and private ambitions could not be read out of existence, but they could be subordinated to higher ends. The harmony of Franklin's New American Order was perfectly consistent with the schema of Madison's *Federalist 10*. The frame of government drafted at Philadelphia was workable because of the breadth of America and the diversity of its members. "Extend the sphere," he wrote, "and you take in a greater variety of parties and interests." In Congress during the 1780's, Madison was continually confronted with

---

[12] John R. Howe, Jr., *The Changing Political Thought of John Adams* (Princeton, 1966), pp. 161-62.

[13] Paul W. Conner, *Poor Richard's Politicks: Benjamin Franklin and His New American Order* (New York, 1965), pp. 11-12, 120, 134-35, 149.

arranging accommodations among group interests. His response in 1788 raised empirical observations to the level of behavioral axioms.

> Those who hold and those who are without property have ever formed distinct interests in society. Those who are creditors, and those who are debtors, fall under a like discrimination. A landed interest, a manufacturing interest, a mercantile interest, a moneyed interest, with many lesser interests, grow up of necessity in civilized nations, and divide them into different classes, actuated by different sentiments and views. The regulation of these various and interfering interests forms the principal task of modern legislation, and involves the spirit of party and faction in the necessary and ordinary operations of the government.

In *Federalist 51* Madison extended his theme: "the security for civil rights must be the same as that for religious rights. It consists in the one case in the multiplicity of interests, and in the other in the multiplicity of sects." By 1792 Madison had elaborated these views into a comprehensive theory of politics.[14]

Such advanced notions did not immediately receive wide acceptance in the new republic, nor in Britain. Christopher Wyvill and the parliamentary reformers hoped to make representation consistent with the presence of interests in society. But many others resisted the dangers inherent in such heresy.[15] Nevertheless, the idea of interest representation became popular in Parliament during the last years of the eighteenth century. "Its attraction lay in the fact that it would be used on all sides; and it did little to detract from the claims of those county reformers who would have been fully satisfied with an increase in the representation of the landed interest. Before very long, Lord North's successors as defenders of the old regime took up

---

[14] *The Federalist* (New York, Modern Library ed.), p. 56; Noble E. Cunningham, Jr., ed., *The Making of the American Party System, 1789 to 1809* (Englewood Cliffs, N. J., 1965), p. 11. See also Madison to Jefferson, 24 Oct. 1787, in Julian P. Boyd, ed., *The Papers of Thomas Jefferson* (Princeton, 1955), XII, 276-79.

[15] Corinne C. Weston, *English Constitutional Theory and the House of Lords, 1556-1832* (London, 1965), p. 155; Black, *The Association*, p. 61.

the principle of interest representation." The new men of power, called Tories, contended that their disagreement with parliamentary reformers was not really a difference of principle; it was merely disagreement over the precise balance desirable in a system of assorted interests.[16]

Actually, the theory of interest representation as it developed before the great Reform Act of 1832 comprehended only a limited number of larger social and economic interests. Nevertheless, the theory was sufficiently flexible to accommodate new interests as they achieved political prominence. Moreover, interests could "offer some share of representation to individuals who obtained no other share." Even so, the classic defense of interest representation, made by Lord Perceval in 1831, showed how closely the system was tied to the distribution of wealth.

> All the interests in society were represented in money, the general representative of value: and as these [rotten] boroughs could be obtained for money, all interests became by these means represented in society. They all found access to Parliament, through that money they all possessed; and so every interest, however it might grow and expand, found access to Parliament, and was represented there.[17]

Because the structures of society in England and America differed, interest representation worked differently and came to mean diverse things in the decades following the American Revolution. In England, the concept and reality were tied to wealth and class. In America, as Thomas Paine noticed in 1791, "by ingrafting representation upon democracy, we arrive at a system of government capable of embracing and confederating all the various interests and every extent of territory and population."[18]

---

[16] J. R. Pole, *Political Representation in England and the Origins of the American Republic* (London, 1966), pp. 453, 526-27.

[17] *Ibid.*, p. 457; *Hansard's Parliamentary Debates*, 3rd ser., III (London, 1831), 266.

[18] Quoted in Roy N. Lokken, "The Concept of Democracy in Colonial Political Thought," *William and Mary Quarterly*, 3rd ser., XVI (1959), 573.

Conflicts between interests rather than between regions or economic classes quickly came to characterize American politics. The notion of representation by interests, however, created a particular problem for the new republic. Men who represented interests were not obliged, even theoretically, to consult for the public good. The most a theorist like James Madison could hope for, in appraising the viability of interest representation, was that the public good would be served by keeping all interests in equilibrium.[19] Unfortunately such a shrewd politician as George Clinton of New York, for example, would use the governor's powers, especially patronage, to build an interest capable of freezing the Federalists out of effective power in the new state.

Consequently, with the dawn of the nineteenth century, men began looking again to government as a guardian of the common interest. The needs and aspirations of special groups became stimuli to direct action, judiciously considered, by the state. In the first half-century of the new republic, the state continued to assume that it was obliged to develop the productive system by favorable legislation, through bounties, monopolies, and acts of incorporation. The significant modification in its role came in the acknowledgment that it ought to make them equally available to all seekers.[20] The public philosophy had grasped and fully transformed the experience of revolutionary America with interest politics.

---

[19] Pole, *Political Representation in England*, pp. 170, 531.

[20] Oscar and Mary Handlin, *Commonwealth. A Study of the Role of Government in the American Economy: Massachusetts, 1774-1861* (New York, 1947), p. 53; Handlin and Handlin, *The Dimensions of Liberty* (Cambridge, Mass., 1961), pp. 72-74.

Bibliographical Essay

Early in the twentieth century, American scholars began to view social activity and political behavior in terms of conflicts among individuals and especially among organized groups. In 1908 Arthur F. Bentley published *The Process of Government,* a profoundly influential work emphasizing the impact of competitive interest groups upon the functioning of government. Charles A. Beard, who also taught at Columbia University, introduced Bentley's work to his graduate students. Beard's distinguished colleagues among historians of the Progressive generation, John R. Commons and Frederick Jackson Turner, shared his conception of political history as a continuing conflict between competing interests.[1] Alfred Thayer Mahan, the widely-read naval historian, stressed competition among national interests in international affairs; and Herbert Croly, a respected journalist and author, believed that "the people" in fact comprised a collection of special-interest groups.[2] Historians and other scholars trained in the tradition of Beard, Turner, and Commons assumed, as Richard Hofstadter recalls, "that the basic motive power in political behavior is the economic interest of groups."[3]

---

[1] John Higham *et al., History* (Englewood Cliffs, N. J., 1965), pp. 178, 180-81.

[2] Eric Goldman, *Rendezvous With Destiny: A History of Modern American Reform* (New York, 1956), pp. 226-27, 338.

[3] Richard Hofstadter, "Status Politics," in Edward N. Saveth, ed., *American History and the Social Sciences* (New York, 1964), p. 191.

Following World War I, however, strong emphasis upon interests in public affairs already seemed naïve. The Progressives had perhaps stressed economic interests to the exclusion of others, and had concentrated unduly upon the role of interests under crisis rather than ordinary conditions.[4] By the time Beard published *The Idea of National Interest* in 1934, he had become highly controversial and in some circles disreputable. Critics of Bentley's work, moreover, began suggesting that decisions of governmental agencies were not always shaped by powerful groups. Governments and their component units could control interests and exercise independent judgment in making policy decisions.[5]

Since the 1950's, however, Bentley's approach to politics has been revitalized and updated by a diverse group of highly sophisticated political scientists. Somewhat more slowly, American historians have come to recognize that the politics of interest, in tandem with other important factors, have dominated certain periods of our past.[6] The third, and crucial, quarter of the eighteenth century was such a period, I believe, and I have analyzed the disruption of the British Empire accordingly.

Ultimately the validity of my interpretation will depend upon subsequent research into many sorts of historical sources. Here I can cite only a few of the many needs and opportunities for further study. The political activities of British mining, metal, and textile industries in the eighteenth century badly need thorough examination. The diffuse shipping

---

[4] Robert E. Osgood, *Ideals and Self-Interest in America's Foreign Relations* (Chicago, 1953), p. 326.

[5] Bernard Crick, *The American Science of Politics* (Berkeley and Los Angeles, 1964), chap. 7; Robert M. MacIver, *The Web of Government* (New York, 1947), p. 220.

[6] See e.g.: Richard Hofstadter, *The Paranoid Style in American Politics and Other Essays* (New York, 1965), pp. 52-53; Harry N. Scheiber, *The Condition of American Federalism: An Historian's View* ([U. S. Senate, 89th Congress, Oct. 15, 1966] Washington, 1966), p. 15; Edward A. Purcell, Jr., "Ideas and Interests: Businessmen and the Interstate Commerce Act," *Journal of American History*, LIV (1967), 561-78.

interests, the Bank of England, and the African interests all require close attention to their political ambitions and operations. The archives of the Hudson's Bay House in London, open to qualified scholars, offer a great treasure of historical documentation for seventeenth-, eighteenth-, and nineteenth-century imperial history.[7] Behind various smuggling and privateering ventures of the eighteenth century were certain financial interests whose identity, organization, and place in British society have not been pinpointed. In sum, a fascinating bit of sleuthing lies ahead for the historical detective.[8]

Students hoping to pursue such researches, and those interested in the complex history of the first British Empire, may wish to begin their studies with some titles from the literature I have described below. "For after all, gentle reader," wrote Washington Irving sardonically, "empires of *themselves*, are nothing without an historian. It is the patient narrator who records their prosperity as they rise—who blazons forth the splendor of their noontide meridian—who props their feeble memorials as they totter to decay—who gathers together their scattered fragments as they rot—and who piously at length collects their ashes into the mausoleum of his work, and rears a triumphal monument to transmit their renown to all succeeding ages."[9]

BIBLIOGRAPHY AND GENERAL REFERENCE

Those seeking to explore imperial history in greater depth should turn first to two bibliographical compilations: Clyde L. Grose, *A Select Bibliography of British History, 1660-1760* (New York, 1967), and Stanley M. Pargellis and J. D. Medley,

---

[7] See Gloria G. C. Harrison, "The Hudson's Bay Company as a Source for North American Research," (Sacramento, Calif., 1965) [Mimeographed Faculty Research Lecture, Sacramento State College].

[8] See the very excellent work by K. R. Andrews, *Elizabethan Privateering: English Privateering During the Spanish War, 1585-1603* (Cambridge, Eng., 1964).

[9] Diedrich Knickerbocker, *A History of New York,* ed. Edwin T. Bowden (New Haven, Conn., 1964), p. 43.

eds., *Bibliography of British History, the Eighteenth Century, 1714-1789* (Oxford, 1951). More recent essays by Robert Walcott, William A. Bultmann, and J. Jean Hecht concerning Stuart and Georgian historiography appear in Elizabeth C. Furber, ed., *Changing Views on British History: Essays on Historical Writing Since 1939* (Cambridge, Mass., 1966), pp. 160-233, along with Philip D. Curtin's "The British Empire and Commonwealth in Recent Historiography," pp. 379-400.

During the eighteenth century the various interests elicited and produced a very considerable literature, ranging from Robert Wilson's briefly titled *The Interest and Trade of Ireland Consider'd* (Dublin, 1731) to the anonymous *Address to the Merchants of Great-Britain: or, A Review of the Conduct of the Administration, with Regard to our Trade and Navigation: shewing how the Trading Interest have been impos'd upon by the Enemies of the Ministry: with a Justification of the Convention concluded between Great-Britain and Spain. By a Merchant retir'd* (London, 1739). All of these fugitive essays and pamphlets have now been catalogued by L. W. Hanson, *Contemporary Printed Sources for British and Irish Economic History, 1701-1750* (Cambridge, Eng., 1963); Henry Higgs, *Bibliography of Economics, 1751-1775* (New York, 1935); J. B. Williams, *A Guide to the Printed Materials for English Social and Economic History, 1750-1850* (New York, 1926), 2 vols.; *Harvard Graduate School of Business Administration, Baker Library; Kress Library of Business and Economics, Catalogue Covering Materials Published Through 1776* (Boston, 1940; and 1955 supplement); Jacob Viner, "Bibliography of English Economic Theory, 1660-1800," *The Cambridge Bibliography of English Literature*, II (Cambridge, Eng., 1941), 957-59.

For the role of mercantile considerations and interest-group activity in Parliament, three major collections of source material should be consulted: Edgar L. Erickson, ed., *British Sessional Papers, House of Commons, 1731-1800* (Readex Microprint); Danby Pickering, ed., *The Statutes at Large from Magna Charta to the End of the Eleventh Parliament of Great*

Britain, Anno 1761, Continued to 1806 (Cambridge, Eng., 1762-1807), 46 vols.; and Leo F. Stock, ed., *Proceedings and Debates of the British Parliaments Respecting North America* (Washington, 1924-41), 5 vols.

For extensive listings of both primary and secondary sources concerning the British Empire in the eighteenth century, consult Lawrence H. Gipson, *The British Empire Before the American Revolution*, XIV-XV (New York, 1969-70), and Bernhard Knollenberg, *Origin of the American Revolution: 1759-1766* (New York, 1960). Jack P. Greene has written a very useful historiographical essay, *The Reappraisal of the American Revolution in Recent Historical Literature* (Washington, D. C., 1967), as well as "The Plunge of Lemmings: A Consideration of Recent Writings on British Politics and the American Revolution," *The South Atlantic Quarterly*, LXVII (1968), 141-75.

SUPPLEMENTARY READINGS

Chapter 1. Introduction: Politics, Mercantilism, and Interests

William E. H. Lecky's *History of England in the Eighteenth Century* (1878-90) moves leisurely through eight volumes. It is fuller for the period after 1760, and particularly good on Ireland. Two recent one-volume studies are sensitive to the role of interests in public life: Dorothy Marshall, *Eighteenth Century England* (London, 1962) and Charles H. Wilson, *England's Apprenticeship, 1603-1763* (New York, 1965). Wilson has also written several important essays concerning mercantilism: " 'Mercantilism': Some Vicissitudes of an Idea," *Economic History Review*, 2nd ser., X (1957), 181-188; "The Other Face of Mercantilism," *Transactions of the Royal Historical Society*, 5th ser., IX (1959), 81-102; and *Mercantilism* (London, 1958), the best brief introduction.

Eli F. Hecksher's *Mercantilism* (2nd ed.; London, 1955), 2 vols., is the classic modern treatment. It should be supplemented by reading several useful essays: Philip W. Buck, *The Politics of Mercantilism* (New York, 1942); Jacob Viner, "Power versus Plenty as Objectives of Foreign Policy in the 17th and 18th Centuries,"

World Politics, I (1948), 1-29; Conyers Read, "Mercantilism: the Old English Pattern of a Controlled Economy," in Conyers Read, ed., *The Constitution Reconsidered* (New York, 1938), pp. 63-78; Bruno Suviranta, *The Theory of the Balance of Trade in England: A Study in Mercantilism* (Helsingfors, 1923), still the best treatment of the subject; and Rudolph C. Blitz, "Mercantilist Policies and the Pattern of World Trade, 1500-1750," *Journal of Economic History*, XXVII (1967), 39-55.

There are several general treatments of the English economy in the seventeenth and eighteenth centuries: E. Lipson, *The Economic History of England*, Vol. II, *The Age of Mercantilism* (6th ed.; London, 1956), stressing the continuity of economic development before and after industrialization, and William Cunningham, *The Growth of English Industry and Commerce in Modern Times: the Mercantile System* (5th ed.; Cambridge, Eng., 1912). Richard Pares has written a fascinating interpretive essay, "The Economic Factors in the History of the Empire," *Economic History Review*, VII (1937), 119-44. Two other essays treat the relationship between colonies and mercantilism: J. F. Rees, "Mercantilism and the Colonies," in J. H. Rose *et al.*, eds., *The Cambridge History of the British Empire* (Cambridge, Eng., 1929), I, 561-602; and Curtis P. Nettels, "British Mercantilism and the Economic Development of the Thirteen Colonies," *Journal of Economic History*, XII (1952), 105-14.

The writings of George Louis Beer, though dated in many ways, still command enormous respect because of the author's diligent research in English archival sources. Beer emphasized the constructive side of English mercantilism, and felt that if it was occasionally misguided, it was not malevolent in intent. Unfortunately Beer did not fully appreciate how mercantile doctrine and practices changed during the seventeenth and eighteenth centuries. *The Origins of the British Colonial System, 1578-1660* (New York, 1908) is followed chronologically by *The Old Colonial System, 1660-1754* (New York, 1912), 2 vols. incomplete, reaching only to 1688, and *British Colonial Policy, 1754-1765* (New York, 1907), which concludes that before 1763 the colonies acquiesced in the laws of trade but criticized some specific provisions; that England and the colonies both made sacrifices for the sake of the empire; and that problems of imperial defense rather than mercantilism caused the American Revolution.

Since Beer the greatest modern authority on the British colonial empire has been Charles McLean Andrews. His two most relevant works are *The Colonial Background of the American Revolution* (New Haven, 1924), and *The Colonial Period of American History*, Vol. IV, *England's Commercial and Colonial Policy* (New Haven, 1938), to which I am very much indebted. Lawrence A. Harper has written the major work on *The English Navigation Laws: A Seventeenth-Century Experiment in Social Engineering* (New York, 1939), while Thomas C. Barrow has provided an important and revisionist volume, *Trade and Empire: The British Customs Service in Colonial America, 1660-1775* (Cambridge, Mass., 1967). The role of the American colonies in the larger context of European politics is treated by Felix Gilbert, *To The Farewell Address: Ideas of Early American Foreign Policy* (Princeton, 1961), Chaps. 1 and 2; and by Max Savelle, *The Origins of American Diplomacy: The International History of Angloamerica, 1492-1763* (New York, 1967), especially Chaps. 5-10, 14-19.

English overseas trade and commercial policies in the early modern period are treated by several authors: Ralph Davis, *A Commercial Revolution: English Overseas Trade in the Seventeenth and Eighteenth Centuries* (London, 1967); G. D. Ramsey, *English Overseas Trade during the Centuries of Emergence* (London, 1957), which concentrates on the sixteenth and seventeenth centuries; C. E. Carrington, *The British Overseas: Exploits of a Nation of Shopkeepers* (New York, 1950); and J. F. Rees, "The Phases of British Commercial Policy in the 18th Century," *Economica*, V (1925), 130-50, which contends that the determinative period in policy-making came during the peaceful years 1713-1739. Statistical compilations and analyses will be found in Sir Charles Whitworth, *State of the Trade of Great Britain in Its Imports and Exports Progressively from the Year 1697* (London, 1776); T. S. Ashton, *Economic Fluctuations in England 1700-1800* (Oxford, 1959); G. N. Clark, *Guide to English Commercial Statistics, 1695-1782* (London, 1938); and Elizabeth B. Schumpeter, *English Overseas Trade Statistics, 1697-1808* (Oxford, 1960).

An understanding of interest politics in Georgian Britain depends very much upon a knowledge of party, faction, and the political process at that time. Several of the most interesting monographs are John Brooke, "Party in the Eighteenth Century," in Alex Natan, ed., *Silver Renaissance* (London, 1961), pp. 20-37; Caroline Robbins, " 'Discordant Parties': A Study of the Acceptance of Party by Englishmen," *Political Science Quarterly*, LXXIII (1958), 505-29; Archibald S. Foord, *His Majesty's Opposition, 1714-1830* (Oxford, 1964); J. H. Plumb, "Political Man," in James L. Clifford, ed., *Man Versus Society in Eighteenth-Century Britain* (Cambridge, Eng., 1968), pp. 1-21; J. Steven Watson, "Parliamentary Procedure as a Key to the Understanding of Eighteenth Century Politics," *The Burke Newsletter*, III (1962), 107-28; and William T. Laprade, *Public Opinion and Politics in 18th Century England* (New York, 1936). Samuel H. Beer has written a brilliant and seminal essay concerning "The Representation of Interests in British Government: Historical Background," *American Political Science Review*, LI (1957), 613-50. *Politics and the Public Interest in the Seventeenth Century*, by J. A. W. Gunn (London, 1969), represents a political scientist's attempt at historical explanation by means of close analysis of texts. He is primarily concerned with the period 1640-1720.

English commercial policies and ideas prior to 1660 may be traced in J. A. W. Gunn, " 'Interest Will Not Lie.' A Seventeenth-Century Political Maxim," *Journal of the History of Ideas*, XXIX (1968), 551-64; R. W. K. Hinton, "The Mercantile System in the Time of Thomas Mun," *Economic History Review*, 2nd ser., VII (1955), 277-90; H. F. Kearney, "Mercantilism and Ireland, 1620-40," *Historical Studies* (London, 1958), I, 59-68; M. P. Ashley, *Commercial Policy Under the Cromwellian Protectorate* (Oxford, 1934); and J. E. Farnell, "The Navigation Act of 1651, the First Dutch War and the London Merchant Community," *Economic History Review*, 2nd ser., XVI (1964), 439-54. The political activity of English and imperial interests before 1660 is explored by John U. Nef, *The Rise of the British Coal Industry* (London, 1932), 2 vols.; L. A. Clarkson, "English Economic Policy in the 16th and 17th Centuries: the Case of the Leather Industry," *Bulletin of the Institute for Historical Research*, XXXVIII (1965), 149-62; Astrid Friis, *Alderman Cockayne's Project and the Cloth Trade* (Copenhagen, 1927); B. E. Supple, *Commercial Crisis and Change in England, 1600-1642: A Study in the Instability of a Mercantile Economy* (Cambridge, Eng., 1959); K. N. Chaudhuri, *The English East India Company: the Study of an Early Joint-Stock Company, 1600-40* (London, 1965); and Robert Ashton, "The Parliamentary Agitation for Free Trade in the Opening Years of the Reign of James I," *Past and Present*, No. 38 (December, 1967), 40-55.

CHAPTER 2. INTERESTS IN EQUILIBRIUM, 1660-1696

There are several valuable treatments of English commerce in the later seventeenth century. An older compendium, still unsurpassed, is by William R. Scott, *The Constitution and Finance of English, Scottish, and Irish Joint-Stock Companies to 1720* (Cambridge, Eng., 1910-1912), 3 vols.; Ralph Davis, "English Foreign Trade, 1660-1700," *Economic History Review*, 2nd ser., VII (1954), 150-66, stresses the spectacular rise of the colonial and reexport trade. The following are also useful: James E. Gillespie, *The Influence of Oversea Expansion of England to 1700* (New York, 1920); Gertrude Z. Thomas, *Richer than Spices* (New York, 1965), treating the growth of the East Indian trade; Sven Erik Åstrom, *From Cloth to Iron: the Anglo-Baltic Trade in the Late 17th Century* (Helsinki, 1963); and by the same author, *From Stockholm to St. Petersburg: Commercial Factors in the Political Relations between England and Sweden, 1675-1700* (Helsinki, 1962), esp. Chap. 3; and M. W. Flinn, "The Growth of the English Iron Industry, 1660-1760," *Economic History Review*, 2nd ser., XI (1958), 144-53.

Relations between commercial interests and government after 1660 are treated by Margaret Priestley, "London Merchants and Opposition Politics in Charles II's Reign," *Bulletin of the Institute of Historical Research*, XXIX (1956), 205-19; R. W. K. Hinton, *The Eastland Trade and the Common Weal in the Seventeenth Century* (Cambridge, Eng., 1959); H. F. Kearney, "The Political Background to English Mercantilism, 1695-1700," *Economic History Review*, 2nd ser., XI (1959), 484-96, is excellent on the lobbying that obtained the Woollen Act of 1699; and Ancil N. Payne, *The Relation of the English Commercial Companies to the Government, 1660-1715* (Urbana, Ill., 1930). Sir John Banks, who governed affairs of the East India Company and the Royal African Company, is the subject of an admirable biography by D. C. Coleman (Oxford, 1963).

The impact of commercial interests upon European diplomacy in these years is discussed in Margaret Priestley, "Anglo-French Trade and the 'Unfavorable Balance' Controversy, 1660-1685," *Economic History Review*, 2nd ser., IV (1951), 37-52; Lawrence B. Packard, "International Rivalry and Free Trade Origins, 1660-78," *Quarterly Journal of Economics*, XXXVII (1923), 412-35; Jacob Price, *The Tobacco Adventure to Russia: Enterprise, Poli-*

tics, and Diplomacy in the Quest for a Northern Market for English Colonial Tobacco, 1676-1722, in Transactions of the American Philosophical Society, new series, LI, Part 1 (Philadelphia, 1961); E. E. Rich, "Russia and the Colonial Fur Trade," *Economic History Review,* 2nd ser., VII (1955) 307-28; Charles Wilson, *Profit and Power: A Study of England and the Dutch Wars* (London, 1957); and G. N. Clark, *The Dutch Alliance and the War Against French Trade, 1688-1697* (London, 1923).

D. A. Farnie synthesized some of the recent literature concerning colonial trade in "The Commercial Empire of the Atlantic, 1607-1783," *Economic History Review,* 2nd ser., XV (1962), 205-18. Bernard Bailyn has offered provocative interpretations of the social structure of Anglo-American commerce in "Communications and Trade: the Atlantic in the 17th Century," *Journal of Economic History,* XIII (1953), 378-87, and *The New England Merchants in the Seventeenth Century* (Cambridge, Mass., 1955). Commercial interests of the far North are treated in E. E. Rich, "The Hudson's Bay Company and the Treaty of Utrecht," *The Cambridge Historical Journal,* XI (1954), 183-203; and in Charles B. Judah, *The North American Fisheries and British Policy to 1713* (Urbana, Ill., 1933). The role of the New World in the politics of interest during the 1680's is highlighted by Albright G. Zimmerman in "Daniel Coxe and the New Mediterranean Sea Company," *Pennsylvania Magazine of History and Biography,* LXXVI (1952), 86-96. The rising importance of the West Indian trade in these years can be traced through the pages of *James Claypoole's Letter Book, London and Philadelphia, 1681-1684,* ed. Marion Balderston (San Marino, Calif., 1967), and K. G. Davies, "The Origins of the Commission System in the West India Trade," *Transactions of the Royal Historical Society,* 5th ser., II (1952), 89-107. Sister Joan de Lourdes Leonard offers some interesting evidence for the tentative coalition of Virginia planters and London tobacco merchants after the Restoration in "Operation Checkmate: the Birth and Death of a Virginia Blueprint for Progress, 1600-1676," *William and Mary Quarterly,* 3rd ser., XXIV (1967), 44-74.

Anglo-American politics in the later seventeenth century are usefully approached through the biographies of prominent practitioners. The Winthrop family has been well served by Richard S. Dunn, *Puritans and Yankees: The Winthrop Dynasty of New England, 1630-1717* (Princeton, 1962) and Robert C. Black, III,

The Younger John Winthrop (New York, 1966), Chaps. 7 and 15. A family specializing in colonial agencies is described by Philip A. Muth, "The Ashursts: Friends of New England," Ph.D. dissertation, Boston University, 1967. William Penn's role and connections are treated by Joseph E. Illick, *William Penn the Politician: His Relations with the English Government* (Ithaca, N.Y., 1965), and Alison G. Olson, "William Penn, Parliament, and Proprietary Government," *William and Mary Quarterly*, 3rd ser., XVIII (1961), 176-95. *The Origins of American Politics* by Bernard Bailyn (New York, 1968) offers an original and thoughtful interpretation. It is misleading, however, in attributing greater stability to interest politics in England than was in fact the case (pp. 100-01).

The Scottish dimension of interest politics may be traced in three monographs: Theodora Keith, *Commercial Relations of England and Scotland, 1683-1707* [Girton College Studies, No. 1] (Cambridge, Eng., 1910); James S. Barbour, *A History of William Paterson and the Darien Company* (Edinburgh, 1907); T. C. Smout, "The Glasgow Merchant Community in the Seventeenth Century," *The Scottish Historical Review*, XLVII (1968), 53-71.

Several useful monographs describe England's colonial policy and administration between 1660 and 1696: P. L. Kaye, *English Colonial Administration Under Lord Clarendon, 1660-67* (Baltimore, 1905); Louise F. Brown, *The First Earl of Shaftesbury* (New York, 1933), Chap. 9; E. E. Rich, "The First Earl of Shaftesbury's Colonial Policy," *Transactions of the Royal Historical Society*, 5th ser., VII (1957), 47-69; A. P. Thornton, *West-India Policy Under the Restoration* (London, 1956); P. S. Haffenden, "The Crown and the Colonial Charters, 1675-1688," *William and Mary Quarterly*, 3rd ser., VI (1958), 297-311, 452-66; and G. H. Guttridge, *The Colonial Policy of William III in America and the West Indies* (Cambridge, Eng., 1922). An important and reliable synthesis will be found in Wesley Frank Craven, *The Colonies in Transition, 1660-1713* (New York, 1968), Chaps. 1-2.

Monographs concerning imperial administrative agencies and their personnel include Charles M. Andrews, *British Committees, Commissions, and Councils of Trade and Plantations, 1622-1675* (Baltimore, 1908); Ralph Paul Bieber, "The British Plantation Councils of 1670-74," *English Historical Review*, XL (1925), 93-106, and *Lords of Trade and Plantations, 1675-1696* (Allentown, Pa., 1919); Michael G. Hall, *Edward Randolph and the American*

Colonies, 1676-1703 (Chapel Hill, N. C., 1960); Gertrude A. Jacobsen, *William Blathwayt, a Late Seventeenth Century English Administrator* (New Haven, 1932); and Stephen S. Webb, "William Blathwayt, Imperial Fixer: from Popish Plot to Glorious Revolution," *William and Mary Quarterly*, 3rd ser., XXV (1968), 3-21.

CHAPTER 3. THE AGE OF WALPOLE, 1696-1748

There are numerous works concerned with English politics during the reigns of Anne and the first Georges. An outstanding work by Geoffrey Holmes, *British Politics in the Age of Anne* (London, 1967) supplants William T. Morgan, *English Political Parties and Leaders in the Reign of Queen Anne, 1702-1710* (New Haven, 1920), and should be supplemented by Henry Horwitz, "Parties, Connections, and Parliamentary Politics, 1689-1714: Review and Revision," *Journal of British Studies*, VI (1966), 45-69. J. H. Plumb has effectively reinterpreted the Age of Walpole and its prelude in *The Origins of Political Stability: England, 1675-1725* (Boston, 1967) and *Sir Robert Walpole* (London, 1956-60), 2 vols. Special studies in this period of English politics include A. J. Henderson, *London and the National Government, 1721-1742* (Durham, N. C., 1942); E. R. Turner, "The Excise Scheme of 1733," *English Historical Review*, XLII (1927), 34-57; and J. Steven Watson, "Arthur Onslow and Party Politics," in H. R. Trevor-Roper, ed., *Essays in British History Presented to Sir Keith Feiling* (New York, 1964), pp. 139-71. Two very different, but equally useful guides to parliamentary politics are by Mary Ransome, "Division-Lists of the House of Commons, 1715-1760," *Bulletin of the Institute of Historical Research*, XIX (1941), 1-8; and James Ralph, *Of the Use and Abuse of Parliaments; In Two Historical Discourses* (London, 1744), 2 vols.

During the first half of the eighteenth century, war and the avoidance of war were major factors in British politics and economic life. A. H. John examines "War and the English Economy, 1700-1763," in *Economic History Review*, 2nd ser., VII (1955), 329-44. C. Earnest Fayle demonstrates the rising importance of interest groups during the 1730's and 1740's in "The Deflection of Strategy by Commerce in the 18th Century," *Journal of the Royal United Service Institution*, LXVIII (1923), 281-90, and "Economic

Pressure in the War of 1739-1748," *ibid.*, pp. 434-46. Also quite valuable for the relationship between government and some interests are H. W. Richmond, *The Navy in the War of 1739-48* (Cambridge, Eng., 1920), and Daniel A. Baugh, *British Naval Administration in the Age of Walpole* (Princeton, 1965).

English involvement in European wars after 1688 profoundly altered the nature of public finance and helped give rise to the moneyed interest during the first half of the eighteenth century. The most important single study is P. G. M. Dickson, *The Financial Revolution in England* (London, 1967), but the student should also consult A. H. John, "Insurance Investment and the London Money Market of the 18th Century," *Economica*, new series, XX (1953), 137-58, and "The London Assurance Company and the Marine Insurance Market in the 18th Century," *ibid.*, XXV (1958), 126-41; and Charles Wright, *A History of Lloyds* (London, 1928), Chaps. 1-7.

A. H. John has also written an important interpretation of "Aspects of English Economic Growth in the First Half of the 18th Century," *Economica*, new series, XXVIII (1961), 176-90, rejecting the customary view that these were years of stagnation in England's foreign trade. Ralph Davis surveys "English Foreign Trade, 1700-1774," in *Economic History Review*, 2nd ser., XV (1962), 285-303, and offers an excellent understanding of "The Rise of Protection in England, 1689-1786," *ibid.*, XIX (1966), 306-17. His most recent work is equally valuable: *Aleppo and Devonshire Square: English Traders in the Levant in the Eighteenth Century* (London, 1967).

There are many good studies of English trade with continental Europe during this period: A. D. Francis, *The Methuens and Portugal, 1691-1708* (Cambridge, Eng., 1966); V. M. Shillington and A. B. Wallis Chapman, *The Commercial Relations of England and Portugal* (London, n.d.), Part II, Chaps. 5-6; H. E. S. Fisher, "Anglo-Portuguese Trade, 1700-1770," *Economic History Review*, 2nd ser., XVI (1963), 219-33; Charles H. Wilson, *Anglo-Dutch Commerce and Finance in the Eighteenth Century* (Cambridge, Eng., 1941), which denotes a shift in Anglo-Dutch interests in the 1730's; J. J. Murray, "Baltic Commerce and Power Politics in the Early Eighteenth Century," *Huntington Library Quarterly*, VI (1943), 293-312; H. S. K. Kent, "The Anglo-Norwegian Timber Trade in the Eighteenth Century," *Economic History Review*, 2nd ser., VIII (1955), 62-74; D. K. Reading, *The Anglo-Russian Commercial Treaty of 1734* (New Haven, 1938); and James G. Lydon, "Fish and Flour for Gold: Southern Europe and the Colonial American Balance of Payments," *Business History Review,* XXXVIII (1965), 171-93.

The political impact of two great trading companies can be seen in P. J. Thomas, *Mercantilism and the East India Trade; an Early Phase of the Protection v. Free Trade Controversy* (London, 1926); Robert Walcott, "The East India Interest in the General Election of 1700-1701," *English Historical Review,* LXXI (1956), 223-39; William T. Morgan, "The Origins of the South Sea Company," *Political Science Quarterly* XLIV (1929), 16-38, and "The South Sea Company and the Canadian Expedition in the Reign of Queen Anne," *Hispanic American Historical Review,* VIII (1928), 143-66; John Carswell, *The South Sea Bubble* (Stanford, Calif., 1960), and Ernest G. Hildner, Jr., "The Role of the South Sea Company in the Diplomacy Leading to the War of Jenkins' Ear, 1729-1739," *Hispanic American Historical Review,* XVIII (1938), 332-41.

Three useful essays on the commercial interest are by J. H. Plumb, "The Mercantile Interest: the Rise of the British Merchant after 1689," *History Today,* V (1955), 762-67; Walter E. Minchinton, "The Merchants in England in the Eighteenth Century," *Explorations in Entrepreneurial History,* X (1957), 62-71; and M. D. McHattie, "Mercantile Interests in the House of Commons, 1710-1713," M. A. thesis, Manchester University, 1949. The silk industry has been examined by Gerald B. Hertz, "The English Silk Industry in the Eighteenth Century," *English Historical Review,* XXIV (1909), 710-27; and Frank Warner, *The Silk Industry of the United Kingdom: Its Origin and Development* (London, [1921]). Michael J. Wise has studied "Birmingham and Its Trade Relations in the Early 18th Century," *University of Birmingham Historical Journal,* II (1949), 53-79.

The development of the Scottish economy in the eighteenth century will be found in R. H. Campbell, *Scotland Since 1707: the Rise of an Industrial Society* (Oxford, 1965), Chaps. 3-4; and "The Anglo-Scottish Union of 1707. II. The Economic Consequences," *Economic History Review,* 2nd ser., XVI (1965), 468-77; Henry Hamilton, *An Economic History of Scotland in the Eighteenth Century* (Oxford, 1963), especially Chaps. 5-14. George P. Insh has made special studies of *The Company of Scotland Trading to Africa and the Indies* (London, 1932), and has edited the *Papers Relating to the Ships and Voyages of the Company of Scotland Trading to Africa and the Indies, 1696-1707* (Edinburgh, 1924), commonly known as the Darien Company. The few essays we have for the Irish interest are excellent: Conrad Gill, *The Rise of the Irish Linen Industry* (Oxford, 1925); Francis G. James, "The Irish Lobby in the Early Eighteenth Century," *English Historical Review*, LXXXI (1966), 543-57; and "Irish Colonial Trade in the Eighteenth Century," *William and Mary Quarterly*, 3rd ser., XX (1963), 574-84.

The burgeoning trans-Atlantic trade during this half-century stimulated the rapid growth of numerous interests concerned with extracting valuable commodities from the New World. Particularly helpful volumes include Ralph G. Lounsbury, *The British Fishery at Newfoundland, 1634-1763* (New Haven, Conn., 1934); Joseph J. Malone, *Pine Trees and Politics, The Naval Stores and Forest Policy in Colonial New England, 1691-1775* (Seattle, Wash., 1964); Murray G. Lawson, *Fur: a Study in English Mercantilism, 1700-1775* (Toronto, 1943); and E. E. Rich, ed., *James Isham's Observations on Hudson's Bay, 1743* ... (Toronto, 1949), as well as Geraldine Meroney, "The London Entrepôt Merchants and the Georgia Colony," *William and Mary Quarterly*, 3rd ser., XXV (1968), 230-44.

Some of the problems posed by colonial manufacturing are discussed in Curtis P. Nettels, "The Menace of Colonial Manufacturing, 1690-1720," *New England Quarterly*, IV (1931), 230-69; E. A. J. Johnson, "Some Evidence of Mercantilism in the Massachusetts-Bay," *ibid.*, I (1928), 371-95; and Keach Johnson, "The Baltimore Company Seeks English Subsidies for the Colonial Iron Industry," *Maryland Historical Magazine*, XLVI (1951), 27-43, as well as "The Baltimore Company Seeks English Markets: a Study of the Anglo-American Iron Trade, 1731-1755," *William and Mary Quarterly*, 3rd ser., XVI (1959), 37-60. Nettels corrects misplaced emphases of George Louis Beer in "The Place of Colonial Markets in the Old Colonial System," *New England Quarterly*, VI (1933), 491-512. Charles M. Andrews has written two important essays concerning "Anglo-French Commercial Rivalry, 1700-1750," in the *American Historical Review*, XX (1915), 539-56, 761-80.

Two outstanding doctoral dissertations shed considerable light on the Anglo-American tobacco trade, especially in the Chesapeake. Jacob M. Price, "The Tobacco Trade and the Treasury, 1685-1733: British Mercantilism in Its Fiscal Aspects" (Harvard, 1954), 2 vols., actually covers the much longer period 1660-1775. Price's work is based largely upon Treasury records, parliamentary journals, and contemporary tracts, and explains how English tobacco merchants tried to avoid the heavy tax burden. See also his article on "The Rise of Glasgow in the Chesapeake Tobacco Trade, 1707-1775," *William and Mary Quarterly*, 3rd ser., XI (1954), 179-99. John M. Hemphill, II, "Virginia and the English Commercial System, 1689-1733" (Princeton, 1964) also keeps the longer period in view. The biographical approach has also been illuminating: see Elizabeth Donnan, "Eighteenth Century English Merchants, Micajah Perry," *Journal of Economic and Business History*, IV (1931), 70-98; Lawrence H. Leder and Vincent P. Carosso, "Robert Livingston (1654-1728): Businessman of Colonial New York," *Business History Review*, XXX (March, 1956), 18-45; and William I. Roberts, III, "Samuel Storke: an Eighteenth Century London Merchant Trading to the American Colonies," *Business History Review*, XXXIX (1965), 147-70. Finally, the emerging commercial interests of the Caribbean may be seen in A. B. Southwick, "The Molasses Act—Source of Precedents," *William and Mary Quarterly*, 3rd ser., VIII (1951), 389-405; Richard B. Sheridan, "The Molasses Act and the Market Strategy of the British Sugar Planters," *Journal of Economic History*, XVII (1957), 63-83, and in A. N. Newman, ed., *The Parliamentary Diary of Sir Edward Knatchbull, 1722-1730* (London, 1963), pp. 86-92.

Robert G. McPherson, ed., *The Journal of the Earl of Egmont: Abstracts of the Trustees Proceedings for Establishing the Colony of Georgia, 1732-1738* (Athens, Ga., 1962); and Amos A. Ettinger, *James Edward Oglethorpe* (Oxford, 1936) both delineate the complicated politicking necessary to the establishment of Georgia after 1730. Trevor R. Reese, *Colonial Georgia: A Study in British Imperial Policy in the Eighteenth Century* (Athens, Ga., 1963) covers Georgia's colonial career succinctly. Comparable studies have been written by W. T. Root, *The Relations of Pennsylvania with the British Government, 1696-1765* (New York, 1912) and George Metcalf, *Royal Government and Political Conflict in Jamaica, 1729-1783* (London, 1965).

Case studies in Anglo-colonial politics during this period are by Michael G. Kammen, "Virginia at the Close of the Seventeenth Century," *Virginia Magazine of History and Biography*, LXXIV (1966), 141-69; John A. Schutz, "Imperialism in Massachusetts during the Governorship of William Shirley, 1741-56," *Huntington Library Quarterly*, XXIII (1960), 217-36; and Stanley N. Katz, *Newcastle's New York: Anglo-American Politics, 1732-1753* (Cambridge, Mass., 1968). Biographical approaches to the politics of imperialism may be taken through Lawrence H. Leder, *Robert Livingston (1654-1728) and the Politics of Colonial New York* (Chapel Hill, N. C., 1961); G. M. Waller, *Samuel Vetch: Colonial Enterpriser* (Chapel Hill, N. C., 1960); J. E. Johnson, ed., "A Quaker Imperialist's View of the British Colonies in America: 1732," *Pennsylvania Magazine of History and Biography*, LX (1936), 97-130; and Roy N. Lokken, "Sir William Keith's Theory of the British Empire," *Historian*, XXV (1963), 402-18.

The various agencies responsible for imperial administration are treated in Oliver M. Dickerson, *American Colonial Government, 1696-1765: a Study of the British Board of Trade in Its Relation to the American Colonies: Political, Industrial, Administrative* (Cleveland, 1912); G. A. Washburne, *Imperial Control of the Administration of Justice in the Thirteen Colonies, 1684-1776* (Washington, 1923); J. D. Doty, *The British Admiralty Board as a Factor in Colonial Administration, 1689-1763* (Philadelphia, 1930); Bernard Pool, *Navy Board Contracts, 1660-1832: Contract Administration Under the Navy Board* (London, 1966); Dora Mae Clark, *The Rise of the British Treasury: Colonial Administration in the Eighteenth Century* (New Haven, 1960); and most recently I. K. Steele, *Politics of Colonial Policy: The Board of Trade in Colonial Administration, 1696-1720* (Oxford, 1968).

In both England and the colonies during these years, the Church of England and various dissenting groups jockeyed for power. Often they were as much involved in public affairs as their commercial counterparts. Norman Sykes has written two helpful studies: *Church and State in England in the Eighteenth Century* (Cambridge, Eng., 1934) and *From Sheldon to Secker: Aspects of English Church History, 1660-1768* (Cambridge, Eng., 1959). More recently T. F. J. Kendrick has examined "Sir Robert Walpole, the Old Whigs and the Bishops, 1733-1736: A Study in Eighteenth-Century Parliamentary Politics," *Historical Journal*, XI (1968),

421-45. Imperial missionary groups have had biographies by H. P. Thompson, *Into All Lands: The History of the Society for the Propagation of the Gospel in Foreign Parts, 1701-1950* (London, 1951), pp. 1-103, and by William Kellaway, *The New England Company, 1649-1776: Missionary Society to the American Indians* (Glasgow, 1961), especially Chaps. 7-10. The politics of dissent have been chronicled by Richard B. Barlow, *Citizenship and Conscience: A Study in the Theory and Practice of Religious Toleration in England During the Eighteenth Century* (Philadelphia, 1962), and Norman C. Hunt, *Two Early Political Associations: the Quakers and the Dissenting Deputies in the Age of Sir Robert Walpole* (Oxford, 1961). The colonial dimension is treated by Maurice W. Armstrong, "The Dissenting Deputies and the American Colonies," *Church History*, XXIX (1960), 298-320; Carl Bridenbaugh, *Mitre and Sceptre: Transatlantic Faiths, Ideas, Personalities, and Politics, 1689-1775* (New York, 1962); and Leonard W. Cowie, *Henry Newman, an American in London, 1708-1743* (London, 1956).

As we have seen, English thinking about political and economic issues shifted gradually between 1696 and 1748. E. A. J. Johnson helps to trace the shift in *Predecessors of Adam Smith: The Growth of British Economic Thought* (New York, 1937), as do Caroline Robbins, *The Eighteenth-Century Commonwealthman* (Cambridge, Mass., 1961), and Jacob Viner, "English Theories of Foreign Trade before Adam Smith," *Journal of Political Economy*, XXXVIII (1930), 249-301, 404-57, although he intentionally omits consideration of colonies in relation to theories of foreign trade. Among prominent men of letters, three of the most interesting are Bolingbroke, Swift, and Defoe. Bolingbroke's intellectual biography is by Sydney W. Jackman, *Man of Mercury* (London, 1965). The *Correspondence of Jonathan Swift*, ed. Harold Williams (Oxford, 1963-65), 5 vols., covering the years 1690 to 1745, makes fascinating reading. John R. Moore has written *Daniel Defoe, Citizen of the Modern World* (Chicago, 1958), but readers should sample this brilliant essayist and publicist themselves. Perhaps the most relevant works to begin with are *An Essay Upon Projects* (London, 1697) and *A Plan of the English Commerce: Being a Compleat Prospect of the Trade of this Nation, as well the Home Trade as the Foreign . . .* (London, 1728).

CHAPTER 4. YEARS OF TRANSFORMATION, 1748-1763

The study of middle Georgian politics must begin with the writing of Sir Lewis Namier, particularly *The Structure of Politics at the Accession of George* III (2nd ed.; London, 1960); *England in the Age of the American Revolution* (2nd. ed.; London, 1961); and [with John Brooke] *The History of Parliament: the House of Commons, 1754-1790* (London, 1964), 3 vols. The condition of the landed interests at this time is best described by G. E. Mingay, *English Landed Society in the Eighteenth Century* (Toronto, 1964) and J. D. Chambers, *The Agricultural Revolution, 1750-1880* (London, 1966).

The ambivalent political circumstances of the working classes may be traced through the works of George Unwin, *The Gilds and Companies of London* (London, 1925), Chaps. 17-19; Edgar S. Furniss, *The Position of the Labourer in a System of Nationalism: A Study in the Labour Theories of the Later English Mercantilists* (New York, 1920); A. W. Coats, "Changing Attitudes to Labour in the Mid-Eighteenth Century," *Economic History Review*, 2nd ser., XI (1958), 35-51; Richard C. Wiles, "The Theory of Wages in Later English Mercantilism," *ibid.*, XXI (1968), 113-26; Eric Bennett, *The Worshipful Company of Carmen of London: A Short History* (Norwich, Eng., 1952), Chaps. 7-8; Margaret Stewart, *The Needle is Threaded. 'The History of an Industry'* (Southampton, Eng., 1964), Chaps. 1-3; J. Steven Watson, *A History of the Salters' Company* (London, 1963), Chap. 4. For a comparison with the colonial situation, see Richard B. Morris, "Labor and Mercantilism in the Revolutionary Era," in Richard B. Morris, ed., *The Era of the American Revolution: Studies Inscribed to Evarts Boutell Greene* (New York, 1939), pp. 76-139.

Urban areas gained considerably in political influence during these years from 1748 to 1763. Their rise is apparent in the essays of Lucy S. Sutherland, "The City of London in 18th-Century Politics," in R. Pares, ed., *Essays Presented to Sir Lewis Namier* (London, 1956), pp. 49-74, and "The City of London and the Devonshire-Pitt Administration, 1756-57," *Proceedings of the British Academy*, XLVI (1960), 147-93. There are several useful works on Bristol: B. D. G. Little, *The City and County of Bristol: a Study in Atlantic Civilisation* (London, 1954), and two volumes edited by W. E. Minchinton for the Bristol Record Society Publications: *The Trade of Bristol in the Eighteenth Century* (1957) and *Politics and the Port of Bristol in the Eighteenth Century* (1963). T. C. Barker has written "Lancashire Coal, Cheshire Salt and the Rise of Liverpool," in *Transactions* of the Historic Society of Lancashire and Cheshire, CIII (1952), 83-101. Still helpful is James Cleland, *The Rise and Progress of the City of Glasgow, Comprising an Account of its Public Concerns* (Glasgow, 1820).

The very important role played by the Bank of England is discussed most recently by J. A. Giuseppi, *The Bank of England: A History from Its Foundation in 1694* (London, 1966). Two major essays are by J. H. Clapham, "The Private Business of the Bank of England, 1744-1800," *Economic History Review*, XI (1941), 77-89, and by D. M. Joslin, "London Private Bankers, 1720-1785," *ibid.*, VII (1954), 167-86. An important parallel study is Armand B. DuBois, *The English Business Company after the Bubble Act, 1720-1800* (New York, 1938).

The changing position of British commercial interests at mid-century appears in many monographs: Jean O. MacLachlan, *Trade and Peace with Old Spain, 1667-1750* (Cambridge, Eng., 1940), Chaps. 4-5; Allan Christelow, "Economic Background of the Anglo-Spanish War of 1762," *Journal of Modern History*, XVIII (1946), 22-36; Eveline C. Martin, *The British West African Settlements, 1750-1821* (London, 1927); R. B. Sheridan, "The Commercial and Financial Organization of the British Slave Trade, 1750-1807," *Economic History Review*, 2nd ser., XI (1958), 249-63; Lucy S. Sutherland, *A London Merchant, 1695-1774* [William Braund] (Oxford, 1933), Chaps. 3-4, and *The East India Company in Eighteenth-Century Politics* (Oxford, 1952); and Earl H. Pritchard, *The Crucial Years of Early Anglo-Chinese Relations, 1750-1800* (Pullman, Wash., 1936). Two doctoral dissertations make special contributions in unexplored areas: Abdul Amir Amin, *British Interest in the Persian Gulf, 1747-1778* (Leiden, 1967) and Serafin D. Quiason, "English Trade Relations With the Philippines, 1644-1765" (University of Pennsylvania, 1962). The critical importance of smuggling in the imperial system and the political influence of smugglers are treated by W. A. Cole, "Trends in Eighteenth-Century Smuggling," *Economic History Review*, 2nd ser., X (1958), 395-410; F. G. James, "Irish Smuggling in the Eighteenth Century," *Irish Historical Studies*, XII (1961), 299-317; and Hohcheung and Lorna H. Mui, "Smuggling and the British Tea Trade Before 1784," *American Historical Review*, LXXIV (1968), 44-73, esp. 70-71.

A few outstanding authors have been responsible for the very clear picture we have of the changing nature of West Indian interests in the 1750's: Lillian M. Penson, "The London West India Interest in the Eighteenth Century," *English Historical Review*, XXXVI (1921), 373-92, and *The Colonial Agents of the British West Indies* (London, 1924); Richard Pares, *War and Trade in the West Indies, 1739-1763* (London, 1936); *A West India Fortune* (London, 1950), Chaps. 9-11; and "The London Sugar Market [1740-69]," *Economic History Review*, 2nd ser., IX (1956), 254-70; Frank W. Pitman, *The Development of the British West Indies, 1700-1763* (New Haven, 1917), and R. B. Sheridan, "The Wealth of Jamaica in the Eighteenth Century," *Economic History Review*, 2nd ser., XVIII (1965), 292-311. See also the stimulating debate over Sheridan's article in *ibid.*, XXI (1968), 30-61.

The condition of North American economic groups is very clearly depicted in James B. Hedges, *The Browns of Providence Plantations* (Cambridge, Mass., 1952); F. B. Tolles, *Meeting House and Counting House: The Quaker Merchants of Colonial Philadelphia, 1682-1763* (Chapel Hill, N. C., 1948); Aubrey C. Land, "Economic Behavior in a Planting Society: the 18th-Century Chesapeake," *Journal of Southern History*, XXXIII (1967), 469-85; C. Robert Haywood, "Mercantilism and Colonial Slave Labor, 1700-1763," *ibid.*, XXIII (1957), 454-64, and "Economic Sanctions: Use of the Threat of Manufacturing by the Southern Colonies," *ibid.*, XXV (1959), 207-19.

Relations between North American and British interests are described in two case studies: R. A. Pelham, "The West Midland Iron Industry and the American Market in the Eighteenth Century," *University of Birmingham Historical Journal*, II (1950), 141-62; Kustaa Hautala, *European and American Tar in the English Market During the Eighteenth and Early Nineteenth Centuries* (Helsinki, 1963). The treatment of North American interests by British ministries during these years is chronicled in Alison G. Olson, "The British Government and Colonial Union," *William and Mary Quarterly*, 3rd ser., XVII (1960), 22-34; Arthur C. Bining, *British Regulation of the Colonial Iron Industry* (Philadelphia, 1933); James P. Ronda, "A Note on the Origins of the Iron Act of 1750," *New Jersey History*, LXXXVI (1968), 171-87; Charles F. Mullet, ed., "A Planter's Protest Against any Additional Tobacco Duty, 1759," *Journal of Southern History*, VIII (1942), 386-92; *A Letter from Mr.* [Thomas] *Knox of Bristol to the Honourable William Nelson, Esq. of Virginia* (Bristol, Eng., 1759), the best source for Bristol's role in lobbying against the tobacco subsidy of 1759; and Thomas C. Barrow, "Background to the Grenville Program, 1757-1763," *William and Mary Quarterly*, 3rd ser., XXII (1965), 93-104.

The intellectual perception of political and economic change at mid-century by contemporaries appears in numerous works. A useful introduction is provided by Wilfrid Harrison, *Conflict and Compromise: History of British Political Thought, 1593-1900* (New York, 1965), Chap. 3. Changes in economic thought are explored by Max Beer, *Early British Economics from the Thirteenth to the Middle of the Eighteenth Century* (London, 1938); G. S. L. Tucker, *Progress and Profits in British Economic Thought, 1650-1850* (Cambridge, Eng., 1960), Chaps. 3-4; William Letwin *The Origins of Scientific Economics* (New York, 1964), Chap. 8. The Scottish Enlightenment produced some of the most perceptive students of British political society at mid-century. See Gladys Bryson, *Man and Society: the Scottish Inquiry of the 18th Century* (Princeton, 1945), Chaps. 6-8; A. S. Skinner, "Sir James Steuart: Economics and Politics," *Scottish Journal of Political Economy*, IX (1962), 17-37; John B. Stewart, *The Moral and Political Philosophy of David Hume* (New York, 1963), a brilliant book; and Shirley R. Letwin, *The Pursuit of Certainty* (Cambridge, Eng., 1965), for valuable material on Hume. The changing use of language is accessible through DeWitt T. Starnes and G. E. Noyes, *The English Dictionary from Cawdrey to Johnson, 1604-1755* (Chapel Hill, N. C., 1946).

There is a great richness of pamphlets and personal views of the 1750's. Several of the most intersting are John Carswell and L. A. Dralle, eds., *The Political Journal of George Bubb Doddington* (Oxford, 1965); Archibald Kennedy, *Serious Advice to the Inhabitants of the Northern Colonies* (New York, 1755); and John Brown, *An Estimate of the Manners and Principles of the Times* . . . (London, 1757; Boston, 1758). The Plumsted Letter Book, 1756-1758, in the Cambridge University Library, has been prepared with an introduction by Ralph Davis for "British Records Relating to America in Microform." Robert Plumsted, a Quaker, London merchant and ironmonger, traded extensively with Philadelphia, Boston, and Barbados. His letters span three important years and reveal the impact of Anglo-American politics on imperial commerce.

CHAPTER 5. AN AGE OF INTERESTS, 1763-1783

The diverse responses of British intellectuals to the problems of the 1760's and 1770's again help to clarify the nature of those problems and the rapidly changing society that was troubled by them. Adam Ferguson, *An Essay on the History of Civil Society, 1767*, ed. by Duncan Forbes (Edinburgh, 1966) extends the analysis of the Scottish thinkers. Two major surveys appeared in the 1770's: Arthur Young, *Political Essays Concerning the Present State of the British Empire . . .* (London, 1772), especially essay 5, and John Campbell, *A Political Survey of Britain: Being a Series of Reflections on the Situation, Lands, Inhabitants, Revenues, Colonies, and Commerce of This Island . . .* (London, 1774), 2 vols., especially II, Book 6.

Adam Smith profoundly affected the outlook of his own and subsequent generations. His ideas and his relations with leading contemporaries are treated by Jacob Viner, "Adam Smith and Laissez Faire," *Journal of Political Economy*, XXXV (1927), 198-232; C. R. Fay, *Burke and Adam Smith* (Belfast, 1956); Thomas R. Eliot, "The Relations Between Adam Smith and Benjamin Franklin Before 1776," *Political Science Quarterly*, XXXIX (1924), 67-96; G. H. Guttridge, "Adam Smith on the American Revolution: an Unpublished Memorial [Feb., 1778]," *American Historical Review*, XXXVIII (1933), 714-20; W. R. Scott, "Adam Smith and the Glasgow Merchants," *Economic Journal*, XLIV (1934), 506-08; and R. Koebner, "Adam Smith and the Industrial Revolution," *Economic History Review*, 2nd ser., XI (1959), 381-91.

The beginnings of the Industrial Revolution in England had unsettling effects upon economic, social, and political life that would be felt throughout the empire. The best introduction is by Phyllis Deane, *The First Industrial Revolution* (Cambridge, Eng., 1965), especially Chap. 13 on "The Role of Government." Particular industries are examined by G. Phillips Bevan, ed., *British Manufacturing Industries* (London, 1876); A. P. Wadsworth and

J. D. Mann, *The Cotton Trade and Industrial Lancashire, 1600-1780* (Manchester, 1931), Chaps. 8-9, 13, 18, 19; and Arthur Raistrick, *Dynasty of Ironfounders: The Darbys and Coalbrookdale* (London, 1953).

Much more relevant to our focus are three recent essays: John M. Norris, "Samuel Garbett and the Early Development of Industrial Lobbying in Great Britain," *Economic History Review*, 2nd ser., X (1958), 450-60; Eric Robinson, "Matthew Boulton and the Art of Parliamentary Lobbying," *Historical Journal*, VII (1964), 209-29; and B. D. Bargar, "Matthew Boulton and the Birmingham Petition of 1775," *William and Mary Quarterly*, 3rd ser., XIII (1956), 26-39. The biographical approach also opens several interesting doors to the study of English commercial life in the 1760's. See Lewis B. Namier, "Brice Fisher, M.P.: A Mid-Eighteenth-Century Merchant and His Connexions," *English Historical Review*, XLII (1927), 514-32, and A. H. John, "Miles Nightingale —Drysalter: A Study in Eighteenth Century Trade," *Economic History Review*, 2nd ser., XVIII (1965), 152-63.

The North of England underwent significant alterations after 1760, and these may be found in Donald Read, *The English Provinces c. 1760-1960: A Study in Influence* (London, 1964), Chap. 1; Francis E. Hyde *et al*, "The Nature and Profitability of the Liverpool Slave Trade," *Economic History Review*, 2nd ser., V (1953), 368-77; W. H. Chaloner, "Manchester in the Latter Half of the Eighteenth Century," *Bulletin of the John Rylands Library*, XLII (1959), 40-60.

Industrial unrest and its political impact during this period is described by R. B. Rose, "Eighteenth-Century Price Riots and Public Policy in England," *International Review of Social History*, VI (1961), pt. 2, pp. 277-92; Eric Hobsbawm, "The Machine-breakers," *Past and Present*, No. 1 (Feb., 1952), 57-70; S. G. E. Lythe, "The Tayside Meal Mobs, 1772-3," *Scottish Historical Review*, XLVI (1967), 26-36; and J. D. Chambers, "The Worshipful Company of Framework Knitters (1657-1778)," *Economica*, IX (1929), 296-329.

The relationship of Irish and Scottish interests to the American crisis is clarified by six very good works: Homer L. Calkin, "American Influence in Ireland, 1760-1800," *Pennsylvania Magazine of History and Biography*, LXXI (1947), 103-20; Maurice R. O'Connell, *Irish Politics and Social Conflict in the Age of the American*

Revolution (Philadelphia, 1965), Chap. 2; Edith M. Johnston, *Great Britain and Ireland, 1760-1800* (Edinburgh, 1963) and "The Career and Correspondence of Thomas Allan, c. 1725-1798," *Irish Historical Studies*, X (1957), 298-324; J. H. Soltow, "Scottish Traders in Virgina, 1750-1775," *Economic History Review*, 2nd ser., XII (1959), 83-98; and M. L. Robertson, "Scottish Commerce and the American War of Independence," *ibid.*, IX (1956), 123-31.

The West Indian interests and their relations with England and the North American colonies are extremely important to an understanding of the coming of Revolution. An older but very helpful essay is by Agnes M. Whitson: "The Outlook of the Continental American Colonies on the British West Indies, 1660-1775," *Political Science Quarterly*, XLV (1930), 56-86. David H. Makinson, *Barbados: A Study of North-American—West-Indian Relations, 1739-1789* (The Hague, 1964), must be used with care. Two very good and complementary books are by Lowell J. Ragatz, *The Fall of the Planter Class in the British Caribbean, 1763-1833* (New York, 1928) and Frances Armytage, *The Free Port System in the British West Indies: A Study in Commercial Policy, 1766-1882* (London, 1953). Allan Christelow has two relevant monographs: "Contraband Trade Between Jamaica and the Spanish Main, and the Free Port Act of 1766," *Hispanic American Historical Review*, XXII (1942), 309-43, and "Great Britain and the Trades from Cadiz and Lisbon to Spanish America and Brazil, 1759-1783," *ibid.*, XXVII (1947), 2-29.

The role of the Caribbean in English displomacy after 1760 is discussed by William L. Grant, "Canada Versus Guadeloupe, an Episode of the Seven Years' War," *American Historical Review*, XVII (1912), 737-43. British policy and peace negotiations at the beginning and end of our period are examined by Z. E. Rashed, *The Peace of Paris, 1763* (Liverpool, 1951); Richard B. Morris, *The Peacemakers* (New York, 1965); and Orville T. Murphy, "The Comte de Vergennes, the Newfoundland Fisheries, and the Peace Negotiation of 1783: A Reconsideration," *Canadian Historical Review*, XLVI (1965), 32-45.

British politics generally between 1763 and 1783 is discussed in J. Steven Watson, *The Reign of George III, 1760-1815* (Oxford, 1960), Chaps. 4-10, and brilliantly in Richard Pares, *King George III and the Politicians* (Oxford, 1953). Herbert Butterfield contributes "Some Reflections on the Early Years of George III's

Reign," *Journal of British Studies,* IV (1965), 78-101. Connections between diplomacy and imperial policy are touched upon in John F. Ramsey, *Anglo-French Relations, 1763-1770* (Berkeley, 1939); Vera Lee Brown, *Anglo-Spanish Relations in America in the Closing Years of the Colonial Era, 1763-1774* (Baltimore, 1923); and John H. Wynne, *A General History of the British Empire in America* (London, 1770), 2 vols.

CHAPTER 6. THE NORTH AMERICAN INTEREST
AND THE IMPERIAL CRISIS

The imperial crisis and ultimate separation of the thirteen colonies from Britain has elicited an enormous literature. I shall suggest only some of the most relevant items here. Readers will find an excellent bibliography in Jack M. Sosin, *Whitehall and the Wilderness. The Middle West in British Colonial Policy, 1760-1775* (Lincoln, Neb., 1961), pp. 269-92, and the most comprehensive coverage in Lawrence H. Gipson, *The British Empire Before the American Revolution,* XIV (New York, 1969). Gipson's extraordinary series, published between 1936 and 1969, stands as a great monument to the diligence and patience of one scholar. I have profited from it immensely. My major interpretive difference with Gipson has to do with chronology and causation. He regards the American Revolution as an outgrowth of "the Great War for the Empire, 1754-63." I have tried to suggest that the political problems which became manifest after 1763 had their origins in the economic and social changes which occurred so rapidly after 1748.

Colonial commerce in the pre-revolutionary era has been carefully appraised by W. T. Baxter, *The House of Hancock: Business in Boston, 1724-1775* (Cambridge, Mass., 1945); Virginia D. Harrington, *The New York Merchant on the Eve of the Revolution* (New York, 1935); Arthur L. Jensen, *The Maritime Commerce of Colonial Philadelphia* (Madison, Wis., 1963); Charles C. Crittenden, *The Commerce of North Carolina, 1763-1789* (New Haven, 1936); Leila Sellers, *Charleston Business on the Eve of the Revolution* (Chapel Hill, N. C., 1934); Charles M. Andrews, "The Boston Merchants and the Non-Importation Movement," *Publications of the Colonial Society of Massachusetts,* XIX (1918), 159-259; Arthur M. Schlesinger, *The Colonial Merchants and the American Revolution* (New York, 1918).

Relations between North American interests and their English correspondents have been explored with especial care for the colony of Virginia. See Lawrence Henry Gipson, "Virginia Planter Debts Before the American Revolution," *Virginia Magazine of History and Biography*, LXIX (1961), 259-77; Joseph A. Ernst, "Genesis of the Currency Act of 1764: Virginia Paper Money and the Protection of British Investments," *William and Mary Quarterly*, 3rd ser., XXII (1965), 33-74; and Walter E. Minchinton, "The Stamp Act Crisis: Bristol and Virginia," *Virginia Magazine of History and Biography*, LXXIII (1965), 144-55. Ernst has also described "The Currency Act Repeal Movement: A Study of Imperial Politics and the Revolutionary Crisis, 1764-1767," *William and Mary Quarterly*, 3rd ser., XXV (1968), 177-211. "The British Credit Crisis of 1772 and the American Colonies," is analyzed by R. B. Sheridan in the *Journal of Economic History*, XX (1960), 161-86. Econometric approaches have been attempted, rather inconclusively, by Robert P. Thomas, "A Quantitative Approach to the Study of the Effects of British Imperial Policy upon Colonial Welfare: Some Preliminary Findings," *ibid.*, XXV (1965), 615-38, and Shepherd, "A Balance of Payments for the Thirteen Colonies, 1768-1772: A Summary," *ibid.*, 691-95.

North American land companies and their interested partisans became significant factors in Anglo-American politics after the Seven Years' War. Thomas P. Abernathy's *Western Lands and the American Revolution* (New York, 1937) must be used along with Sosin, *Whitehall and the Wilderness*, cited earlier. Shaw Livermore, *Early American Land Companies: Their influence on Corporate Development* (New York, 1939) provides an introduction to the histories of particular groups: A. P. James, *The Ohio Company: Its Inner History* (Pittsburgh, 1959); A. P. James, *George Mercer of the Ohio Company: A Study in Frustration* (Pittsburgh, 1963); Peter Marshall, "Lord Hillsborough, Samuel Wharton and the Ohio Grant, 1769-1775," *English Historical Review*, LXXX (1965), 717-39; J. P. Boyd, "The Susquehannah Company, 1753-1803," *Journal of Economic and Business History*, IV (1931), 38-69; George E. Lewis, *The Indiana Company, 1763-98* (Glendale, Calif., 1941); and especially two very useful biographical studies, Nicholas B. Wainwright, *George Cronghan: Wilderness Diplomat* (Chapel Hill, N. C., 1959), Chap. 10, and Sewall

E. Slick, *William Trent and the West* (Harrisburg, Pa., 1947), Chap. 11.

Alongside the land-company lobbyists, the largest group representing North American interests in London before the Revolution consisted of the various colonial agents and merchants trading to America. They are treated by Jack M. Sosin, *Agents and Merchants: British Colonial Policy and the Origins of the American Revolution, 1763-1775* (Lincoln, Neb., 1965), and by Michael G. Kammen, *A Rope of Sand: The Colonial Agents, British Politics and the American Revolution* (Ithaca, N. Y., 1968). The bibliographical essay in my book includes a comprehensive listing of all previous literature concerning the colonial agents. Other "innocents abroad" are discussed by William L. Sachse, *The Colonial American in Britain* (Madison, Wis., 1956).

Several authors have concerned themselves with the impact of British politics upon the coming of the Revolution. One of the best is G. H. Guttridge, *English Whiggism and the American Revolution* (Berkeley, Calif., 1942). Two complementary volumes, with surprisingly little overlap, are Charles R. Ritcheson, *British Politics and the American Revolution* (Norman, Okla., 1954) and Dora Mae Clark, *British Opinion and the American Revolution* (New Haven, 1930). More recently there have been special studies by Allen S. Johnson, "The Passage of the Sugar Act," *William and Mary Quarterly*, 3rd ser., XVI (1959), 507-14, and "British Politics and the Repeal of the Stamp Act," *South Atlantic Quarterly*, LXII (1963), 169-88, and by Bernard Donoughue, *British Politics and the American Revolution, The Path to War, 1773-1775* (London, 1964).

Some of the most readily accessible primary sources for this period are filled with illustrations of the themes discussed in Chapter 6. See "Debates on the Declaratory Act and the Repeal of the Stamp Act, 1766," *American Historical Review*, XVII (1912), 563-86; Lawrence H. Gipson, ed., "The Great Debate in the Committee of the Whole House of Commons on the Stamp Act, 1766, as Reported by Nathaniel Ryder," *Pennsylvania Magazine of History and Biography*, LXXXVI (1962), 10-42; Basil Williams, "Chatham and the Representation of the Colonies in the Imperial Parliament," *English Historical Review*, XXII (1907), 756-58; William Knox, *The Interests of the Merchants and Manufacturers of Great Britain, In the Present Contest with the Colonies, Stated and Considered* (London, 1774); Josiah Tucker, *A Letter to Edmund Burke, Esq., . . . In Answer to His Printed Speech, Said to Be Spoken in the House of Commons on the 22nd of March, 1775* (Gloucester, 1775).

The initiation and implementation of British colonial policy between 1763 and 1775 is one of the most thoroughly researched topics in all of American historiography. Policy-making in London, or the search for a policy, is the subject of two articles by Robin A. Humphreys: "Lord Shelburne and the Proclamation of 1763," *English Historical Review,* XLIX (1934), 241-46, and "Lord Shelburne and British Colonial Policy [1766-68]," *ibid.,* L (1935), 257-77; as well as Neil R. Stout, "Goals and Enforcement of British Colonial Policy, 1763-1775," *American Neptune,* XXVII (1967), 211-20, and three essays by Jack M. Sosin, "A Postscript to the Stamp Act: George Grenville's Revenue Measures. A Drain on Colonial Specie?" *American Historical Review,* LXVIII (1958), 918-23, "Imperial Regulation of Colonial Paper Money, 1764-1773," *Pennsylvania Magazine of History and Biography,* LXXXVIII (1964), 174-98, and "The Massachusetts Acts of 1774: Coercive or Preventive?" *Huntington Library Quarterly,* XXVI (1963), 235-52.

The institutional origins of colonial policy may be traced through Arthur H. Basye, *The Lords Commissioners of Trade and Plantations . . . 1748-1782* (New Haven, 1925); Franklin B. Wickwire, *British Subministers and Colonial America, 1763-1783* (Princeton, 1966); Margaret M. Spector, *The American Department of the British Government, 1768-1782* (New York, 1940); B. D. Bargar, *Lord Dartmouth and the American Revolution* (Columbia, S. C., 1965); and Dora Mae Clark, "The American Board of Customs, 1767-1783," *American Historical Review,* XLV (1940), 777-806.

Two controversial and related issues concern the impact of the Navigation Acts on the colonists and the question of whether there really was a change in policy after 1763. Contradictory answers will be found in Frederic J. Ericson, *The British Colonial System and the Question of Change of Policy* (Chicago, 1943); Lawrence A. Harper, "The Effect of the Navigation Acts on the Thirteen Colonies," in Richard B. Morris, ed., *The Era of the American Revolution. Studies Inscribed to Evarts Boutell Greene* (New York, 1939), pp. 3-39; Oliver M. Dickerson, *The Navigation Acts and the American Revolution* (Philadelphia, 1951); Edmund S. and

Helen M. Morgan, *The Stamp Act Crisis: Prologue to Revolution* (Chapel Hill, N.C., 1953); Benjamin Woods Labaree, *The Boston Tea Party* (New York, 1964).

Many other Anglo-colonial controversies, only slightly less inflammatory than the Stamp Act crisis and the tea party, are discussed by Jack P. Greene, *The Quest for Power: the Lower Houses of Assembly in the Southern Royal Colonies, 1689-1776* (Chapel Hill, N. C., 1963), and "Bridge to Revolution: the Wilkes Fund Controversy in South Carolina, 1769-1775," *Journal of Southern History*, XXIX (1963), 19-52; and by Francis G. Walett, "Governor Bernard's Undoing: an Earlier Hutchinson Letters Affair," *New England Quarterly*, XXXVIII (1965), 217-26.

The larger setting of the American Revolution must take into account European diplomacy and the reorientation of English imperial thinking and interests. Richard Van Alstyne has done the former compactly in *Empire and Independence: The International History of the American Revolution* (New York, 1966). *Benjamin Franklin and American Foreign Policy*, by Gerald Stourzh (Chicago, 1954), is a suggestive analysis. Before his untimely death Vincent T. Harlow had virtually completed his monumental set, *The Founding of the Second British Empire, 1763-1793* (London, 1952-1964), 2 vols. The separate volumes are subtitled *Discovery and Revolution* and *New Continents and Changing Values*. Harlow's thesis that the second empire was already developing before the first collapsed has stimulated scholars to rethink many conventional assumptions about imperial history. See Peter Marshall, "The First and Second British Empires: A Question of Demarcation," *History*, LIX (1964), 13-23; Marshall, "The British Empire and the American Revolution," *Huntington Library Quarterly*, XXVII (1964), 135-45; G. C. Bolton, "The Founding of the Second British Empire," *Economic History Review*, 2nd ser., XIX (1966), 195-200; Ronald Hyam, "British Imperial Expansion in the Late 18th Century," *The Historical Journal*, X (1967), 113-24.

EPILOGUE: YET ANOTHER TRANSFORMATION

The impact of the American Revolution on British imperial ideas and realities was considerable. The most immediate considerations are analyzed by David Fieldhouse, "British Imperialism in the Late

18th Century," in A. F. Madden, ed., *Essays in Imperial Government Presented to Margery Perham* (Oxford, 1963), pp. 23-45; R. Coupland, *The American Revolution and the British Empire* (London, 1930); David S. Reid, "An Analysis of British Parliamentary Opinion on American Affairs at the Close of the War of Independence," *Journal of Modern History*, XVIII (1946), 202-21; Charles R. Ritcheson, "The American Revolution: Its Influence on the Development of the British Empire," *Parliamentary Affairs*, IV (1951), 245-60. The long view is appraised by Robert L. Schuyler, *The Fall of the Old Colonial System: A Study in British Free Trade, 1770-1870* (New York, 1945), and Helen Taft Manning, *British Colonial Government After the American Revolution, 1782-1820* (New Haven, 1933). Implications of the Revolution for Canada are surveyed by G. S. Graham, *British Policy and Canada, 1774-1791* (London, 1930), and Chester Martin, *Empire and Commonwealth: Studies in Governance and Self-Government in Canada* (Oxford, 1929). Donald N. Winch describes the new attitudes toward colonies, from Adam Smith to John Stuart Mill, in *Classical Political Economy and Colonies* (Cambridge, Eng., 1965).

While the War for American Independence was still in progress, English reformers began seeking changes in the structure of government, representation, and public finance. Their attempts, some unsuccessful and others requiring years for fulfillment, are detailed in Ian R. Christie, *Wilkes, Wyvill, and Reform: The Parliamentary Reform Movement in British Politics, 1760-1785* (London, 1962); Eugene C. Black, *The Association: British Extraparliamentary Political Organization from 1769 to 1793* (Cambridge, Mass., 1963); John Norris, *Shelburne and Reform* (London, 1963); John E. D. Binney, *British Public Finance and Administration, 1774-1792* (Oxford, 1958); and A. Aspinall, *Politics and the Press, c. 1780-1850* (London, 1949).

Relations between British commercial interests and the government after the Revolution are developed in John Ehrman, *The British Government and Commercial Negotiations With Europe, 1783-1793* (Cambridge, Eng., 1962); Witt Bowden, "The Influence of the Manufacturers on Some of the Early Policies of William Pitt," *American Historical Review*, XXIX (1924), 655-74; Bernard Semmel, "The Hume-Tucker Debate and Pitt's Trade Proposals," *The Economic Journal*, LXXV (1965), 759-70; and B. W. Higman,

"The West India 'Interest' in Parliament, 1807-1833," *Historical Studies* [University of Melbourne], XIII (1967), 1-19. The fortunes of the East India Company during these years are carefully examined by C. H. Philips, "The East India Company 'Interest' and the English Government, 1783-84," *Transactions of the Royal Historical Society*, 4th ser., XX (1937), 83-101; and by Holden Furber, "The United Company of Merchants of England Trading to the East Indies, 1783-1796, *Economic History Review*, X (1940), 138-48.

The fur trade provided an important reminder after 1783 of Britain's former commercial interests in North America. Aspects of the continued significance of the fur trade will be found in Gordon C. Davidson, *The North West Company* (Berkeley, 1918); Louise P. Kellogg, *The British Regime in Wisconsin and the Northwest* (Madison, Wis., 1935); N. V. Russell, *The British Regime in Michigan and the Old Northwest, 1760-1796* (Northfield, Minn., 1939).

Changes in the quality and character of American economic life before and after the Revolution are discussed in two highly thoughtful essays by George R. Taylor, "American Economic Growth Before 1840: an Exploratory Essay," *Journal of Economic History*, XXIV (1964), 427-44, and by Gordon C. Bjork, "The Weaning of the American Economy: Independence, Market Changes, and Economic Development," *ibid.*, 541-60. Changes in American political thought appear in two excellent studies: Paul W. Conner, *Poor Richard's Politicks: Benjamin Franklin and His New American Order* (New York, 1965), and John R. Howe, Jr., *The Changing Political Thought of John Adams* (Princeton, 1966).

The Comparative Dimension

Many of the trends and problems I have noted in the first British Empire are paralleled, literally or obversely, in other contemporary colonial systems. The student might begin with Earl J. Hamilton, "The Role of Monopoly in the Overseas Expansion and Colonial Trade of Europe Before 1800," *American Economic Review*, XXXVIII (1948), 33-53. Hamilton has treated "Spanish Mercantilism Before 1700," in *Facts and Factors in Economic History* (Cambridge, Mass., 1932), pp. 214-39. Clarence H. Haring, *Trade and Navigation Between Spain and the Indies in the Time of the*

Hapsburgs (Gloucester, Mass., 1964) considers each of the major facets of mercantilism, as does José Larraz, *La Época de Mercantilismo in Castilla, 1500-1700* (Madrid, 1943). C. R. Boxer describes *Portuguese Society in the Tropics: the Municipal Councils of Goa, Macao, Bahia, and Luanda, 1500-1800* (Madison, Wis., 1965), and W. J. Van Hoboken examines "The Dutch West India Company; the Political Background of Its Rise and Decline," in J. S. Bromley, ed., *Britain and the Netherlands. Papers Delivered to the Oxford-Netherlands Historical Conference* (London, 1960), pp. 41-61. In *The Genesis of German Conservatism* (Princeton, 1966), Klaus Epstein observed that "the materials presented suffice . . . to substantiate the point that German Conservative thought and action was from its beginning [*c.* 1770-1806] closely connected with particular political and economic interest groups" (vii).

Charles W. Cole has written *French Mercantilist Doctrines Before Colbert* (New York, 1931) and *Colbert and a Century of French Mercantilism* (New York, 1939), 2 vols.; he concludes that in Colbert's day private interests in France had less influence in shaping mercantile policy and measures than private interests in England. Other useful studies include Stewart L. Mims, *Colbert's West India Policy* (New Haven, 1912); Paul W. Bamford, *Forests and French Sea Power, 1660-1789* (Toronto, 1956); Lionel Rothkrug, *Opposition to Louis XIV: The Political and Social Origins of the French Enlightenment* (Princeton, 1965), Part 2; J. F. Bosher, *The Single Duty Project. A Study of the Movement for a French Customs Union in the Eighteenth Century* (London, 1964), especially Chap. 3; Daryl M. Hafter, "Critics of Mercantilism in France, 1751-1789: the Industrial Reformers" (Ph.D. dissertation, Yale University, 1964); and Marcel Giraud, "France and Louisiana in the Early Eighteenth Century," *Mississippi Valley Historical Review*, XXXVI (1950), 657-74. Among the physiocrats, perhaps the most representative view of the proper relationship between the national interest and particular commercial interests will be found in Le Mercier de la Rivière, *L'Ordre Naturel et Essentiel des Sociétés Politiques* (1767: Paris, 1910), especially pp. 27, 155, 267-68.

Political Science: Theoretical and Empirical

Among the theoretical and analytical approaches to the role of interest groups in political systems, I have most benefitted from

Gabriel A. Almond, "A Comparative Study of Interest Groups and the Political Process," *American Political Science Review*, LII (1958), 270-82, and Francis G. Castles, *Pressure Groups and Political Culture: A Comparative Study* (London, 1967). Other valuable essays include Roy C. Macridis, "Interest Groups in Comparative Analysis," *Journal of Politics*, XXIII (1961), 25-45; W. J. M. MacKenzie, "Pressure Groups: the 'Conceptual Framework,' " *Political Studies*, III (1955), 247-55; and Alfred de Grazia, "Nature and Prospects of Political Interest Groups," *Annals of the American Academy of Political and Social Science*, CCCXIX (Sept., 1958), 113-22.

Efforts to describe and analyze the importance of interests in contemporary America have their modern genesis in David B. Truman's *The Governmental Process: Political Interests and Public Opinion* (New York, 1951). The attitudes of political scientists toward interest group behavior have changed so rapidly in the past fifteen years that one literally needs a catalogue of the various viewpoints. The most useful brief guide will be found in Theodore J. Lowi, "American Business, Public Policy, Case Studies and Political Theory," *World Politics*, XVI (1964), 677-715. Harmon Ziegler has updated Truman's work in some respects in *Interest Groups in American Society* (Englewood Cliffs, N. J., 1964).

Three writers have made the most important contributions to the study of interests in British political society. S. E. Finer has prepared *Anonymous Empire: A Study of the Lobby in Great Britain* (London, 1958) and "Interest Groups and the Political Process in Great Britain," in H. W. Ehrmann, ed., *Interest Groups on Four Continents* (Pittsburgh, 1958), pp. 117-44. W. J. M. Mackenzie defines and classifies types of "Pressure Groups in British Government," in the *British Journal of Sociology*, VI (1955), 133-48, and Allen M. Potter has written *Organized Groups in British National Politics* (London, 1961). An entire issue of *The Political Quarterly*, XXIX (1958), no. 1, was given over to a symposium concerning "Pressure Groups in Britain."

Index